Extreme Europe

TOPOGRAPHICS

Extreme Europe

Stephen Barber

REAKTION BOOKS

This book is dedicated to Catherine.

Published by Reaktion Books Ltd
79 Farringdon Road, London EC1M 3JU, UK

www.reaktionbooks.co.uk

First published 2001

Printed and bound in Great Britain by
Biddles Ltd, Guildford and King's Lynn

British Library Cataloguing in Publication Data

Barber, Stephen
   Extreme Europe. – (Topographics)
   1. Europe – History 2. Europe – Civilization 3. Europe –
   Description and travel
   I. Title
   914

   ISBN 1 86189 091 5

Contents

Introduction

The transformation of Europe in the years after the fall of the Berlin Wall brought an entirely new dynamic to the continent's visual culture. While much of that culture has been homogenized, a more vital and disruptive culture exists on the peripheries. This is a contemporary urban culture which draws upon everything from digital images and graffiti to the more archaic but nonetheless resonant filmic and photographic images engrained in the memory of Europe's cities by its histories of conflict and atrocity. Despite its vivid forms, that peripheral culture often lies buried within the superficial urban environment that encloses Europe's inhabitants, numbing their perception. The aim of this book is to explore the multiple dimensions of those border zones of Europe and their cultures: the interlinked extremes of geography, imagery, sexuality, architecture, political power, national obsession – the extremes of cities and of the human body itself.

This book takes the form of a series of journeys around the peripheries of Europe and its cities, via a number of the areas from which the defining moments and images of contemporary Europe have been generated. On such journeys, the primary impression is of the great upheaval that has taken place in the media culture of Europe over recent years, especially the way in which this upheaval has overhauled the surfaces of cities by means of digital-image screens, signs and hoardings and proliferating visual façades of every kind. Throughout Europe, that omnipresent culture and its screens direct themselves towards consumer images and their grip on their spectators. Out on the extremes of Europe, however, it is sometimes possible to catch glimpses of ways in which those screens are being contested by a culture compacted from tenacious, even indelible images suffused by Europe's torn past. On the peripheries, those originating images themselves constitute a kind of aberrant, oppositional screen – often in a state of disintegration but no less compelling for that – which exists in tension with the rising saturation of dominant media and corporate cultures. The essential fascination of a journey through the extremes of Europe lies in the possibility of witnessing that visual confrontation and especially its impact on the inhabitants of cities.

Each of the journeys described in this book has its own distinct trajectory and aims. The route and direction of the first one, around the far perimeters of Europe, are, to some extent, as arbitrary and capricious as the assigned borders of Europe themselves. This journey is designed to investigate sites that project the power its borders exert on those living both inside and outside them. At some points, the permeable appearance creates a volatile overlap with exterior cultures, while at other points, the perimeters are rigidly enforced as an intractable barrier.

The second journey traverses Berlin, extending across the revealing division between the twentieth century's end and the new century's beginning. The fact that Berlin lies towards the centre of the geographical expanse of Europe works contrarily, to both reinforce and exacerbate its key role as the site from which many of the twentieth century's most extreme – often lethal – ambitions and systems of power emerged, encompassing human, architectural, cultural and historical dimensions. In Europe, the centre and the extreme are deeply entangled. Contemporary Berlin also forms the arena in which the urgent conflict between an

8

engulfing but insipid form of media power and the surviving traces of more momentous images is at its most crucial, with the outcome of that struggle pointing directly into the future of Europe's visual culture.

The final journey involves a sequence of explorations around the suburbs of Paris. Paris is unique in the tightly bordered nature of its inner districts, whose celebrated landmarks and boulevards possess a fabulous aura. This part of the book intentionally ignores those familiar landmarks in order to investigate less-known terrain, which is in many ways more captivating, inhabited as it is largely by a population of exiles who have come to envision a very different future for European culture than that planned within its central spaces.

Peripheries of Europe

Europe begins and ends at any point you want it to. Any direction travelled leads to another periphery. The journey could be oblique or direct, broken into jump-cuts or continuous: eventually, it will bring the eye up close against the edges of Europe. Any limit reached demands another interrogation, of the body in Europe, of its nations and cities, and of its sexual and media cultures. A decade after the fall of the Berlin Wall and the start of the vast transformations and upheavals this event engendered, I decided to explore the four extreme corners of Europe, to try and seize what lay inside them.

I first travelled east from England. Whatever the speed and means of the journey, by road, rail or foot, the traversal of north-western Europe gives the impression of a euphoric flying, with occasional plummetings into cities. The last traces of England give out and the North Sea engulfs the eye. The presence of northern European seas and lakes permeates the journey with a permanent crossing of water, the divisions between sea and land oscillating in grey and ochre flickers. Many of the cities on that journey – Amsterdam, Hamburg, Helsinki – are so immersed and centred in their attachment to the sea that they also appear tenuously braced against the potential of being swallowed up by it. The cities hold themselves in tension around the water's edge, and their inhabitants breathe a contrary, energized air that contains all the deep decay that the sea brings, in intimacy, to the land. But the sea also transfuses great wealth into the cities at its edge, as it has for many centuries, with each site weighed down by the grandiose municipal architecture of its central squares. The back alleyways are sunken, too, but in an alcoholic stupor enlivened by the rapid gestures of drug transactions and bursts of violence.

Punctuated by abrupt rashes of cities, the north-western European plain veers towards the horizon in infinite tracts of farmland and webs of railway lines that extend all the way to the Urals. The traveller's initial euphoria turns to an awareness of atrocity as it traverses this terrain. Across the centuries, from one direction or another, this land was intermittently crossed and scorched by armies of occupation, with populations massacred or displaced and cities destroyed. At one time or another, across twenty centuries, almost every city across north-western Europe suddenly ignited in conflict like a match. If these cities were to be observed from a point high above them, through a time-compressed lens, those ignitions might look as though they had been designed and activated by a particular intention to create an intricate arrangement of urban fire. Over the first half of the twentieth century, the density of that arrangement would have grown to virulent splendour and then extinguished itself suddenly over the second half, in anticipation of its next outburst. Like the spectacular panorama of burning oil wells left behind in Kuwait by the retreating Iraqi army in 1991 – filmed from above in streams of flame shooting up from the desert surface – the landscape of north-western Europe now appears as a sensitive ground primed for conflagration, only thinly overlayered and made to adhere by its affluence and complacency. Media and advertising images erupt from its cities. Their inhabitants move around in a snared daze, from supermarket to department store, within streets walled by blazing media screens.

The expanse of consumer delirium that lies spread out before the eye across the icy cities of northern Europe's plains and seacoasts is only gritted by those that have been too dec-imated, too ground into the earth, to adopt such a vulnerable passivity. The wry unease and obstinacy of their inhabitants often takes the form of sexual cultures. In Hamburg, espe-cially – where the air was whipped up by firebombing in 1943 to a temperature of a thousand degrees, with over 50,000 inhabitants incinerated in one air-raid alone – the membrane between lust and extinction is at its most porous; only in such a city of overpowering deliberation could the extreme caprice of sexual experimentation slip through and take the dominant hand. The sensory matter of the city tracks its way from deep heat to intense cold and back again, and every resilient fibre of that matter holds an awareness of potential sudden reversal or elimination within it. On a night walk through the resonating marine air of Hamburg, from the restlessly crammed sex alleys and clubs to the empty squares of unwieldy civic buildings, the city's stubborn per-versity unleashes itself on the eye.

Heading towards Poland, the plain of Europe buckles, scarred by the glowering presence of eastern Germany. Whenever I criss-crossed eastern Germany in the years imme-diately after the fall of the Berlin Wall, every journey revealed absence and desperation. The supplanted communist state, the German Democratic Republic, had encompassed chronic pollution, mass surveillance and suppression, but at least it had held its insanity together. Its industry and infrastructure were abruptly gutted, and eastern Germany became a land of the dispossessed, the disintegration of its intricate life style replaced by a void. From the Baltic port cities down to Leipzig and Dresden, the GDR's inhabitants received a raw shock to the head. Even at that moment, the invasive power of the West German Federal Republic possessed the aura of a corrupt act of inveiglement, its extent only becoming fully visible a decade later. A ludicrous conjuring trick made the GDR disappear at the drop of a hat, to be replaced by a pile of soiled banknotes, of dubious origin, which vanished equally rapidly. Ten years on, the peripheral landscapes of the former GDR remained scattered with innumerable concrete tenements, cracked in zigzags from bottom to top, surrounded by stalls selling low-grade spirits to groups of addled men immersed in silent paralysis; the walls bore the decaying layers of neo-fascist graffiti that had begun to accumulate almost as soon as the GDR had dematerialized. Tenement blocks were being renovated to a pristine pitch of homo-geneity, but every pair of eyes staring out from them still appeared concussed, its gaze detached from itself. The inhabitants had accustomed themselves to living in a zone of banality, caught in the suspended animation of a compulsive dance of media images.

From the eastern side of the Oder, the immense terrain of north-eastern Europe opens out across Poland and Russia. All the way to the Urals, between dispersed cities of crumbling buildings and jarring tramways, the land is once again studded with traces of atrocity, inflicted more intensively than in north-western Europe: the acts of genocide, the expulsions and pogroms that characterize the last vestiges of Europe. Only the boundary of the Urals finally annuls those traces. The act of flying over those mountains brings a strong sense of abandonment, even relief: Europe is over, and far beneath the form of the Aeroflot jet lost in the searing blue sky, Siberia stretches away towards the Pacific, across vast mountain ranges and steppes inscribed by the elliptical language of ox-bow lakes, the fragile thread of the trans-Siberian railway being the only human intrusion upon infinite swathes of blank surface. But even at that far perimeter, Europe refuses to give out completely, gripping with subzero tenacity in the gradually emptying Stalinist 'pioneer' cities, such as Vorkuta, where the passionate exceeding of industrial quotas, in the middle decades of the twentieth century, marked yet one more aberrant excess in Europe's history. At every extreme corner, Europe seeps irrepressibly over its own boundaries; only the corporeal sensation engendered by the speed and disintegration of the journey can create a tangible form for it.

From the frozen corner of north-eastern Europe, the journey along its eastern edge takes the form of a jagged descent. This journey progresses in fits and starts, switch-backing and dead-ending; the eyes, too, are prey to the dynamic of spasms and abrupt reversals. If you believe that you are moving ahead for a moment, you know that an obstacle is imminent. The route by train is often blocked for days on end in some isolated rural town where the peasants inch by in roughly made wooden carts, pulled along dirt roads by steaming horses or dogs. Europe appears petrified. At its perimeters, it often seems that the very time of Europe has wound down and stalled, and is even beginning to career in reverse. Photographs of such sites from a century ago would exactly match the most contemporary images of the same locations, right down to the oblique eyes of their human faces. And with every step, another scar is unearthed in the terrain. Whenever the journey acquires momentum for a moment, the sense of a euphoric flight over a terrain of atrocity returns, only to crash abruptly. Everywhere, the rare, crawling trains fill to overflowing with the intimidated human figures, wrapped in black shawls and ragged overcoats, who always amass in the zones where lives have been locked down through one system or another for centuries, and where the primary gesture of cities is one of ferocious and disdainful expulsion.

On a journey through the countries of eastern Europe, the cities pass by in an engulfing medium of concrete façades, human affront and industrial cacophony, with their main avenues over-illuminated at night by glaring orange street lighting and the rawest consumer images. In the main plazas, eroded monuments erected during the post-war decades – devoted to dictators and heroes, to massacres and victims – come together in neglect, jammed alongside one another, their exposed iron substructures visible beneath pitted surfaces of obscene graffiti. The inhabitants appear restless, the effects of unrelenting consumer paroxysms apparent in each facial muscle.

Though every memory is irreparably transformed into illusion by nostalgia, I had a different impression whenever I travelled southwards through eastern Europe in the years immediately following the collapse of the communist regimes. A strange calm had descended on the cities there: the vertiginous feeling of those days had left behind them a moment almost of bliss, with the inhabitants' eyes pooled in the collective anticipation of a vacant future that would never arrive. It always seemed to be the end of summer or early autumn in those moments, whatever the actual time of year. A dry, translucent mist hung in the dusty streets, and the tram tracks shimmered in sunlight below the wrecked façades of tenements still bullet-incised from the end of the war. And at night, the avenues were silent, unlit except for glowing 1950s neon signs, the names of empty cinemas pulsing outwards in curved letters of violet and emerald light.

As the journey moves southwards, the cities gradually become more affluent, the populations less swamped by the effects of a multigenerational malediction on their lives.

Some of the cities bear traces of the mass tourism that traversed eastern Europe at the beginning of the 1990s, in a reverse direction to the great movements of emigration that had originated in the same cities in the nineteenth and early decades of the twentieth centuries, movements towards more secure western European cities, such as Paris, or out beyond the confines of Europe altogether. The throng of wealthy young tourists from the United States, Australia and Canada followed a crooked vector that passed from west to east through a succession of momentarily fashionable cities, from Prague to Sofia to Constanza. The crumbling boulevards of previously insulated cities carried suddenly international populations, crazed with lust and open-mouthed with awe. In Prague, the greatest concentration of that grafted population – a hundred thousand strong at its maximal point – amassed within a fabulous strip of prosperous bars and cafés, a strange, ephemeral apparition alongside grimy streets devoted to long-ingrained routines of hard drinking and prostitution. By the end of the decade, that young population had largely dispersed, leaving behind a debris of derelict bars and blaring English-language signing. The surfaces of these cities had shaken slightly as they absorbed their itinerant human influx and then disregarded it as just another minor ripple on the surface of eastern Europe, which has always been marked by rapid traversals of populations and cultures. Few tenaciously rooted eastern European cultures exist; each remaining population has somehow become locked in transience, lacking the momentum to emigrate and somehow eluding the twentieth century's invasions and deportations. Only the stasis of endurance permanently inhabits these areas.

In eastern European cities, the compulsion to gaze is always countered by its reversal in a subjection to abrasive scrutiny. Around Keleti railway station in Budapest, the accumulation of directed gazes becomes searing as innumerable pimps and hustlers minutely scan every arriving traveller. Throughout the city, the oscillating points of focus and subjection are assembled with an ever-greater concentration, collecting in its maximum intensity on Váci utca. The avenues of Budapest have possessed a uniquely transmutating visual style for over a century, forming densely impacting exclamations of visual image and written matter, of light and darkness: in the forms of advertising hoardings, café and shop signs, posters and displays. Now, as those visual surfaces rot and bloom simultaneously – with digital images supplanting disintegrating neon texts – the system of power enacted within the streets will aggressively rob the eye of all individual focus. Throughout the cities of eastern Europe, this ocular experience can be both an abysmal and a pleasurable loss: the city's core is certainly a site where the immersing of the senses in its images provokes an ecstatic dissolution of vision.

Moving from city to city, I saw the hold that a vast consumer culture of homogenization had taken on the surfaces of eastern Europe's streets and on the eyes of its inhabitants. When the first traces of that culture were emerging, a decade ago, I had thought that its inept forms would soon be discarded. But its contagion quickly spread and consolidated itself, extending from the central corporate plazas to the far peripheries. In every alleyway, and behind every bar and restaurant, a furtive transaction of shoddy or narcotic goods is perpetually taking place, in a cellular-phone exchange of mutters and refusals. The moment when the call is abruptly cut off, in a tense stand-off, marks the successful conclusion of the transaction. The present time and space of eastern Europe are relentlessly condensed, their transformations signalled by sudden movements of abandonment without transition. Any sustaining myth of the city can no longer be carried through to its fulfilment: all narratives of human growth or regeneration now belong to the media of the cities' consumer culture, with those narratives' intricate shapes brutally concertina'd into the glaring immediacy of the void.

Towards the south-eastern angle of Europe, the cities become more tentatively grounded. The solidity of the northern European metropolises is infinitely far away, and the journey progresses more through a scattered diffusion of urban gestures rather than via direct trajectories across defined terrains. Everywhere, shabby cities are battered together from substandard concrete-casting, their inhabitants jammed together within cracked structures. In the early morning and late evening, vast gatherings of isolated figures collect around tram stops, each one certain that it is both valid and obligatory to wait, indefinitely if necessary. But when the groaning trams arrive, the act of waiting becomes the most intolerable thing conceivable, and elbows and curses fly until the carriages are filled to bursting point and the trams reel away to the city centre, or else back to the far-flung suburbs, with their axis in shopping plazas and alcohol stores. The interval between the stasis of waiting and the unleashing of movement is an agonizing boundary of life in the suburbs. The railway stations too are crammed, the wooden benches colonized as though seized for use over generations, the vast and echoing waiting halls blackened with many decades of tobacco smoke. Every traveller has a range of objects to treasure, to check, to hold on to – especially at night, when any relaxation is instantly punished by theft. Every now and then, station announcements crackle, but the sound is so loud and damaged in transmission that the waiting populations must disassemble and piece its elements together like organs in a botched autopsy.

The train jolts to a standstill in the dead of night, at a darkened platform beneath the ruins of a majestic station carapace, constructed under a long-gone imperial system. The next train will not leave until dawn. For a few hours, you walk the streets of a provincial city to which you know you will never return: in some cities, late-night hustlers are still in futile overdrive, but in others, inhabited only by lassitude, you pass by without a single eye tracking your momentary traversal of their streets. As you approach the extreme points of south-eastern Europe, the single-line railway tracks give out altogether, and the only solution is to take a decrepit bus – a brakeless vehicle protected only by glittering icons and crucifixes, and crowded with rural passengers who must surely have a mission to travel, however indecipherable it may be – through mountain valleys, to reach the next starting point of the railway line. Only the desire to finally escape from exhaustion propels you forward. You promise yourself to give up travelling but keep travelling.

In Albania, the cities fall apart before your eyes. By that point in the journey around Europe, any euphoria generated by the compulsive act of travelling has disintegrated too, so that the matter of the peripheral cities asserts itself in all its raw, contrary detail. When I travelled through Albania immediately after the end of its communist regime – which had kept the country isolated for decades, so that it formed an enigmatic void on every map of Europe – the cities and landscapes appeared enmeshed in a state of lethargy. At that moment of abrupt transition, the country was literally lawless, all its social structures razed to the ground. Every half-finished building had been abandoned, all cultivation arrested, all shipping and fishing suspended. It seemed that the very will for survival was being interrogated by the entire country; at such a moment of extremity, nothing could have appeared so attractive as the utter surrender of all intention. Beyond the struggle against total poverty, there lay the shimmering prospect of that ecstatic capitulation. The powerful forces of lassitude form perimeters that mark out Europe, capable of magisterially overruling its illusions, its intricate media power and all of its images. Only the agitated ten-year-old children of the Albanian cities seemed to be determinedly searching for a new starting point, and they put their trust in a tenuous miracle. They told me: 'We are waiting for the USA to save us.' They gnashed their teeth in hunger and exhilaration, their gaze of intent speculation searching for any sign of life, any escape.

From the windows of threadbare buses without timetables, in 1991, I had watched long files of children by the roadside, walking for hours to reach the only bakery in their district, to return with an immense loaf of sawdust bread – itself almost the same size as a child's malnourished body – that would have to last a family until the rare energy for another such trek had been accumulated. A few members of the population had been able to travel to more affluent countries to work at menial jobs and had brought back tenth-hand German cars. The emptiness of the pitted roads seemed to induce an uncontrollable desire for lethal speed, and wrecked cars could be seen overturned in ditches, having spun out of control and simply been left there to rust. When rioting broke out in the southern city of Saranda, four years later – after the arcane 'pyramid' savings scams had collapsed – I had read about a demonstration at which there had been pleas for an end to the elated shooting of guns, since a number of children had been killed accidentally. The crowd yelled its approval for the pleas, the cries accompanied by the wild shooting of guns. Nothing could come closer to revealing the intimate logic of Europe's peripheries.

Almost a decade on from its zero point, Albania had finally grown calmer, though the intractable fissure in its substance maintained an uneasy presence in the cities, now newly encased in shoddy tenements almost indistinguishable from those spread out, in jumbled satellites, across the entire eastern European landscape. The brutal Albanian mafia networks of prostitution and drug-dealing, extending throughout Europe and operated by men who would now have been the same age as the America-dreaming children I had encountered in 1991, had created an erratic influx of sudden wealth for parts of the country. In the extreme south, at the abandoned city of Butrinte, I felt that I was reaching into the angle of another far corner of Europe. The waterlogged peninsula, surrounded by purple lakes and the Adriatic, carried the layers of many civilizations that had successively inhabited the city across centuries – fighting over it in power struggles, abandoning it in lassitude, revivifying it and infusing it with splendour – until its foundations finally sank too deeply into the surrounding waterlands and it was left permanently to decay. I reached the lost city on a bus that had left Saranda at dawn. All around me, the mountains of southern Albania were holding up a fierce black sky of storms whose rain never fell. Along the coast, terraces of olive plantations had long fallen into disuse. But further on, beside a broken-down chain-ferry that crossed the estuary close to Butrinte, affluent villas were now being constructed on the sites of former collective farms. During my previous visit, the ragged children of the collective farms on the far bank had collected at the water's edge to gaze at the empty city. That city remained deserted and silent. I fought my way through the overgrowth covering the ruins, past the Roman forum and up the hill to the derelict castle that looked out in all directions, onto a vast landscape of sea, ruined city and mountain. The sky was immense and open while, down below, the city lay with all of its pounded-down, cancelled cultures and empires. From this site emanated the sensation of being at the far end of the world, let alone of Europe.

Europe moves in convulsions, from poverty to affluence (at the end of the 1990s, Butrinte became a World Heritage Site and began to absorb vast sums of money for excavation work), from conflagration to satiation and back again; it is a terrain that can only pass from extremity to extremity. It veers from the astonishing panorama that can open all boundaries to the minuscule detail of dirt ingrained in the eager eyes of the children of its abandoned cities.

On the passenger ferry that crosses the water between Istanbul and Üsküdar in Turkey, nobody is searching for the border between Europe and Asia that must be situated, intangibly, at some point of that crossing. For all of the passengers, traversing the Bosphorus is simply a banal journey from one part to another of a colossally sprawling city whose flailing suburban arms extend in all directions. Istanbul forms the most unworkable city at the edges of Europe and is all the more intensely inhabited for its sheer impossibility. Swathes of human figures perpetually course up and down its hills, blocking the paths of huge yellow shared taxis, crammed to their battered and split sides with passengers. Alongside the streaming crowd, their peripheral component of shrunken, crippled or aged bodies, bundled into black clothing, stumbles tenaciously along. The act of living is not surrendered easily on that far perimeter. Istanbul is in a permanent state of demolition and reconstruction, but it stretches out too vastly, its decomposition and neglect are too deeply rooted, for any perceptible improvement ever to be made.

From the ferry, the Bosphorus reflects a sky cushioned, at low altitude, by an immense heat-haze of pollution that starts to gather in the early morning and disperses only momentarily at night. On the ferry, the old men standing among the ancient wooden benches exchange stories in rapid sequences of evocation, silence and exclamation. Young boys walk around with trays loaded with minuscule glasses of hot tea, urns strapped to their backs. The ferry's funnel sends its own minor contribution up into the great dirty heaven above the city. After a few minutes, Istanbul moves away into the distance, and the broken-down media screens and exclamatory advertising hoardings amassed above the Rihtim Caddesi intersection disappear from sight. The visual hold of the city's terminally congested slopes of mosques and other buildings slips away completely as the ferry nears the centre of the Bosphorus. If a clear limit existed to Europe, a defined point of exit or entry, it would be here, but the prospect of that boundary being discernible swiftly evanesces in the blaring delirium of voices, among the dense inter-crossing of sea traffic.

As the ferry arrives at Üsküdar, the air becomes perme-ated with the smell of grilled fish, handed out by fishermen from tiny boats moored at the quayside. Stepping down from the ferry, you place your feet on an ostensible Asia,

which possesses its own slippery evasions from any limits imposed upon it. The air is calm, the cardiac frenzy of Istanbul superseded. People of all ages sit in the cool shade on the Üsküdar esplanade doing nothing at all. Time's urgent passage is suspended, at least for the moment.

Further down the coast, however, many of the far suburbs that supply millions of manual workers daily to Istanbul's centre have been devastated, their concrete apartment blocks nonchalantly thrown to the ground by the effects of earthquake shocks on the built-in flaws of their inept construction, their inhabitants crushed inside. Those decimated city-satellites lie under a polluted sky that itself seems to be gasping for survival. I take another ferry further down through the Sea of Marmara; from the coast, the south-eastern suburbs extend as far as the eye can absorb them. If the Bosphorus does indeed mark a kind of finishing line for Europe, those infinitely replicated concrete suburbs are exterior to Europe. They possess the aura of exhausted long-distance runners who have gone too far, passing beyond the finishing line, unable to stop, until their legs seismically go from under them. The edges of Europe are cruel to whatever falls outside them.

I left the ferry at its terminus, on the island of Büyükada, where an utter silence filled the air. Inside the ferry terminal, its dome still surmounted by the obsolete insignia of the Ottoman Empire, prowling cats inhabited the waiting rooms, with not a human face in sight. For centuries, the island had served as the zone of expulsion for Istanbul's political dissidents and undesirable elements. In the early decades of the twentieth century, it had become the chosen home for an intricate mix of different populations, including many of Istanbul's Jewish inhabitants. The stretch of sea between the island and the city created a fragile protective barrier, and the inhabitants of Büyükada could look on with a certain detachment as Turkey's governments oscillated across the century between Islamic and European culture, each perceived as the other's extreme opposite. The island grew wealthy and fashionable, but by the end of the century, even the safety net of the sea had appeared to diminish; the islanders found themselves becoming increasingly vulnerable to the seething political, religious and national conflicts of south-eastern Europe. Most of them departed for more secure locations, and the wooden villas and houses were left to disintegrate.

Walking through the derelict and emptied alleyways of Büyükada – an island poised between Europe and Asia – I wondered whether this was how Europe itself would end: annulled in the aftershocks of conflicts over national obsessions at its boundaries, in the wake of escalating bouts of religious violence and territorial warfare. For most of the inhabitants of Europe, as they watch their televisions, such conflicts become bloodless and diluted, existing almost entirely within the arena of media images whose impact is undiminished by its lack of visceral content; Europe is driven to the edge by diverse means, sluiced away down a drain composed of both media images and brutal conflicts. In those tranquil alleyways, however, populated almost entirely by gangs of cats, any concern with the future of Europe could not be sustained for long. The island inspired a merciful oblivion in its few visitors. No motorized vehicles were allowed, and horse-drawn carriages travelled at low speed along roads of rich black dirt. Up on the densely wooded hills, the island's isolated monasteries were also serenely inching their way towards disintegration. When occasional faces appeared in the town, they seemed blithe and relaxed. For a few weeks in the summer, at least, a degree of activity would return, and the shuttered casino and hotel would open up to a transient, international clientele. Istanbul remained invisible from the island, though when a thunderous rain poured down, it was tainted with the city's hot and bitter taste.

On a journey westwards across the southern limits of Europe, you move from island to island, and the sea opens up endlessly before you. The physical trial of eastern Europe dispels itself, and the sun sears away exhaustion. The huddled, frozen presences who haunted the excoriating public spaces of eastern Europe, their lives pulverized into submission, now form a distant memory; in southern Europe, the cities' inhabitants display capricious gestures of assertion. The washed-out grey façades of the northern cities transmute into colours that appear almost hallucinatory by contrast: strong azures and burning reds. After the severity of its northern zones, the southern cities of Europe appear to possess no desire to maintain their autonomy from other cultures, and assemble their elements almost by accident, concocting them into lithe arrays of images and languages that can metamorphose effortlessly, without any visual wrench. The limits of Europe, on its southern peripheries, often seem to be marked out by a line that barely sustains a continuous pressure on the map, so that in places, around islands scattered across the Mediterranean, they appear to glide, zigzag or even make no mark at all. But such an impression is a heat-fuelled illusion, and at points along that margin, such as the southern coast of France, the fearful line is pressed down with an ultimate hostility, incised indelibly.

Southern Europe seethes in its myths and stories, but its pre-eminent narratives amass around the matter of the origins of Europe itself. The myth of Europe begins – and ends – in an act of violence: the abduction of Princess Europa, carried away by the disguised king of the gods, Zeus, while she was gathering flowers on the beach at her home in Tyr, and taken west across the ocean to Gortyn, on the central plain of Crete. There, on the hot earth beneath a plane tree, Europa and Zeus engaged in a frenzied originating sexual act, a hundred years in duration, to engender the children who could carry the myth of Europe forward, towards power and conflict.

In southern Europe, myths transform themselves compulsively into histories and actions. I reached Gortyn by a crammed bus on a day of pounding heat. It was the only bus of the day on a narrow road from the northern to the southern coasts of the island, and I watched market-bound peasants gesturing wildly, in dismay, at the driver as he sped by them in deep concentration on the way ahead. The crucifixes and icons attached by rosary beads to the opaque rear-view mirror reeled from side to side. The driver overshot the unmarked Gortyn stop, but then reversed, sending the peasants standing in the aisle flying forwards. The site of Gortyn was isolated within a parched plain of olive groves and banana plantations, resonating with layers of insect noise. I climbed over the broken stone wall that surrounded the deserted site. Dust flew up from the ochre ground: no rain had fallen for weeks, and the site emanated an aura of utter stasis. Down towards a barely running stream, the ancient plane tree – beneath which the first great sexual act in the existence of Europe was asserted to have taken place – stood half-heartedly cordoned off within a boundary of low fencing. Europe, at the core, is a contrary matter of dust and semen, its southern perimeters marked out fluidly by narratives and myths of lust and death. Every story of its origins is finally as bogus as it is intricate – a sequence of delusional fabrications about how a contested entity established its authority – but any such story of sensorial impact is worth more than a multiplicity of void images.

Waiting by the roadside at Gortyn, in the evening heat of a cicada cacophony, for the bus back to the northern coast, I wondered about the likelihood of its actually stopping for me. All around, lost within the dense overgrowth, the ruins of the vast, annulled Roman city of Gortyn, whose power had once encompassed all of the territories of northern Africa, lay hidden from view. When the bus arrived, it pulled over adroitly to the roadside, empty apart from a 90-year-old woman carrying a goat on her lap. The site of Gortyn was instantly obscured from sight by the dust churned up from the bus's skidding back wheels, and the traces of its myth of the origins of Europe, in lust and abduction, were swallowed back into oblivion. But the contemporary cities of southern Europe still operate by means of parallel strategies: the terraces of the seafront boulevards form great arenas of intense sexual gazing at twilight, each young body visually seized and pinioned by the eyes of other bodies, and male public toilet stalls resonate with the half-expelled screams and gasps of furtive sexual acts.

To the scanning eye, the southern extremes of Europe melt into space: they shift and appear porous. While the northern cities are unremittingly evident – their presence ground by atrocity into the very earth – the southern ones wheel into and then fade from sight: they operate within the realm of peripheral vision, their essential substance compounded from figments and mirages, placed just outside the range of vision. I took one last ferry ride to try to pin down the edge of southern Europe, through the act of standing on its southernmost point: the island of Krissi, off the coast of southern Crete. But that island turned out to be a site that possessed no cohering mass whatsoever. It formed an unstable, ephemeral smear of livid silver sand and scrubland that threatened to vanish with the slightest rise in sea level. The weekly ferry from the port of Ierapetra reluctantly crossed the intervening stretch of sea, its decrepit planks screeching against the currents, and docked at the island's ramshackle jetty. A few ragged inhabitants got on and off; the island had no houses, only a few sparse huts thrown together from sea-storm debris, half-submerged in thick thorn bushes and whipped by hot ocean winds. From the southern tip of the island, the Mediterranean stretched away towards the coast of Libya. I swam out southwards above the coral, surrounded by shoals of tiny fish; as I looked back towards the island, it appeared flattened out almost to invisibility, its fragility reinforced by the raw white mountains of mainland Crete towering behind it. Without the tangible presence of any defining land or space to focus on, the only means to gauge that extreme boundary of southern Europe exactly must be corporeal. In swimming as far out as you can, to the point of exhaustion, you finally reach the far limits of Europe.

Along the Mediterranean coast of Italy and then into France, the line of affluent apartment blocks and retirement villas scours its way westwards, almost unbroken even in soaring mountainous terrain, for hundreds of miles along the oceanfront. But that homogeneous façade of Europe is irreparably fissured by the city of Marseilles, whose abrupt manifestation forms a howling detonation of life and dirt. Most of the population of northern France views this city with deep suspicion as the epitome of crassness, infested with racism and corruption. Marseilles has been dubbed 'the dustbin of Europe', as though the function of the river Rhône were to pick up all the massed detritus of Europe from a central point of collection in Switzerland and transport it directly to that abject terminus. Inversely, the inhabitants of the city itself wear t-shirts declaring themselves 'Proud to be from Marseilles'. On the quayside of the Old Port, a plaque grandly ascribes to Marseilles the status of being the originating site from which all western European civilization developed, that origin calculated arbitrarily as the arrival of the city's Phocaean settlers. All around that origin-of-Europe, the wild inhabitants scream and gesture as boats setting out for the islands in the bay prepare to leave. From the quayside, rushing upwards in every direction, Marseilles pursues its ferociously vocal existence through elegant, tree-lined central boulevards, all the way out to its high-tension concrete suburbs, until only a solid wall of white mountain rock finally manages to curtail the irrepressible city. In Marseilles, the peripheral visual screen of Europe becomes a vastly open zone that magnetizes everything in its sight, then sends that violently scrambled mass of images, languages and sensations pouring back out again into the streets. Marseilles exudes the glaring, vital indignity of Europe.

On the boulevards, wisecracking gangs of girls in platform boots and minuscule black dresses glare at boys in
loosely hanging leisurewear of every colour under the sun.
The lunatic spasms and tics which animate the city are
accentuated by the blasts and moans of the Mistral, the
wind whose aim is to wreak a mad havoc upon its inhabitants. But the integral lunacy of the city alternates with a
deep, sustaining calm, as though the full insanity of Europe
were a known, accepted quantity in those precipitate streets.
And if that knowledge were in fact to be the originating
point for a conception of Europe, it would certainly be one
infused with a liberating sense of reality. During the
wartime occupation of Marseilles, its Old Port district of
Le Panier proved so maniacally unruly and subversive to
the regime of the German forces that they razed all of its
overflowing alleyways to the ground. But this had no
effect, since that oppositional tenacity was able to survive
any supposed annihilation of its surfaces. The city evades
all oppressive restriction, moving and acting uncontrol-
lably and articulating itself in a multitude of ways. In the
evenings, voluble groups and gangs of every age congregate

in the squares and on tree-shaded corners, everyone speaking at once, stragglers feverishly elbowing their way into the mass of bodies in order to make themselves heard.

The great sensory rush of the city's noise is silenced only from the terrace of the basilica of Notre Dame de la Garde, on its hill far above the white buildings and boulevards. The walk up to the basilica is a hard climb, through twisting alleyways of decrepit houses, neighbourhood bakeries shuttered against the afternoon sun and replaced by long-broken bread-vending machines. Only the insane would make such a journey in the Marseilles heat. A nun is there to bless you as you complete your miraculous ascent. The basilica's walls remain lacerated by machine-gun fire from the fierce fighting of August 1944 for the liberation of the city. From that summit, the city appears strangely tamped down, caught between the immense perspectives of the mountains and the sea. Out on the ocean, ferries from Oran, Algiers and Tunis head unhurriedly towards the docks at its western edge, their decks glittering in the white-hot light. Within the city, the vast, sculpted stone stairway of Saint-Charles railway station is visible, forming another majestic entrance to the city. Around that station, at street level, the city's infinite sexual and narcotic transactions are pursued in their dense detail of gestures and outbursts. But for one contrary moment, from the rarefied heights of the basilica, the imposing panorama of Marseilles appears austere and splendid, as though it could be the great originating city of European civilization after all. Once you leave it behind and continue west, though, its memory is enough to stun you with consternation.

The far corner of south-western Europe forms a merciless zone for those who are compelled to test the permeability of its boundaries. Over the dangerous stretch of turbulent sea between Tangiers and the southern tip of Spain, any illicit traversal by boat makes for a precarious ride, and the dawn beaches carry the open-mouthed, cold corpses of poverty-stricken boys from north Africa whose illusions about Europe have proven to be terminal. That dreaming traversal abruptly comes up against an intractable barrier of thin air far more deadly than the leaded cloud of pollution that hangs over the Bosphorus between Europe and Asia. From the heights of Tangiers, Africa and Europe seem locked in confrontation, staring nose-to-nose at one another.

For a time in the early 1950s, at the bitter end of Morocco's colonization, the human debris of Europe sprawled so expansively across Tangiers that the city almost overlapped with Europe, taking the form of a bizarre outcrop of its aberrations. At that time, half of the city's population was made up of exiles attracted by its proliferating sexual cultures, together with masses of eastern European refugees and corrupt entrepreneurs. From the luxuriant garden terraces of the Grand Hôtel Villa de France, high up on the city's hillside, the narrow sea channel – out towards the extremes of Europe – must have appeared as negligible but essential to their lives, momentarily reprieved from the seizure of Europe. By the early 1990s, the palatial hotel had transformed itself into a mediocre brothel, falling finally into dereliction. The grimy boulevards of Tangiers gathered an aura of urgent unease. The city's European population had vanished, and the view out across the Straits of Gibraltar was cut with a murderous edge. Sometimes, on its far peripheries, it seems that everything Europe touches turns to dust.

Storms and gales amass and roar at the point where the

western Mediterranean is strangled into extinction, and the vast gaping eye of Europe opens out onto the Atlantic Ocean. The far end of the Mediterranean disgorged most of the fifteenth century's great experiments, via the medium of sea exploration, into a vision that expanded beyond Europe. That need to engender a new space beyond the confines of Europe remains an imperative urge for those of its mutinous inhabitants who perceive it as an arena of visual subjection or powerful constraint. Throughout its imperial history, every aspiration to expand Europe disintegrated or was crushed, and all such ambitious schemes were irresistibly transformed from the grandiose to the risible. In the end, all that survives are the enduring, contrary determinations to both escape from and enter Europe's shimmering limits; those incendiary desires come together to generate a pure, searing light at its south-western boundaries.

In Lisbon, that light is at its most concentrated, and the city forms a dizzying concoction of dense darknesses and glaring illuminations. In its shadows, the inhabitants are elusive presences; in that city of precipices and abrupt elevations, everyone is up one minute, down the next. The city's tramways – the most outdated of which were built in the north of England, in the vanished steelworks of Yorkshire – appear always to take the most tortuous and convoluted routes through its disorientating alleyways, which seem to head in every opposing direction simultaneously. On the European periphery, few cities form sensory experiences that can be easily assimilated; Lisbon contorts the eyes and body exactingly in order to anchor itself corporeally in the consciousness of its inhabitants. At every far corner of Europe, intimacy with incipient calamity is sinewed into the hearts of cities; Lisbon carries that flaw within itself, from its destruction by earthquake in 1755 to its conflagration in 1988.

38

In such an ether-pumped atmosphere, any kind of urban upheaval can soon be absorbed, as was the revolution of 1974 which cast off an inane military junta. Lisbon possesses an old, intently aware eye that watches transformations pass by. Even in its contemporary architectural apparitions – such as the vast silver blocks and pink crenellations of the Amoreiras commercial complex, which towers in jarring extravagance above the swathes of decrepit tenements – the city appears archaic to the core. Europe, too, subsists in its deeply ingrained obsolescence, even while its digital-image screens flare in all their immediacy.

In rua Augusta, one of the ornate pedestrian avenues that lead down from Rossio Square to the Tagus riverfront, a ragged boy of two or three sat cross-legged every day in the middle of the stream of fast-moving human legs, playing a tiny accordion and singing a song without words. The only element of the song was the sound 'aa-aa', each articulation rendered differently, from two abrupt gulps to endlessly drawn-out sighs. His child's voice moved from one expiration to another like an ancient mouth at the point of death, protesting at agony in fear or snarling in derision, slow and then fast, fast and then slow, for as long as the respiratory tract could hold out. Lisbon's ramshackle inner-city areas are inhabited almost entirely by great gangs of children, moving energetically in blurred masses of flying limbs and cries down the slopes of the Alfama district. The few adult faces in those veering alleyways appear absent and effaced, and project no sensation. Alongside the children, and moving much more slowly, stooped and aged figures wrapped tightly in black clothing grip the iron handrails in the centres of the alleyways to make their infinitesimal descent. The city cannot mediate between its extreme populations: life moves abruptly from youth to old age, with no intervening span.

At that expiring point of Europe, the sea pours in to annul the land. Europe is on its last legs. Out to the west of Lisbon, past the suburb of Cascais, I stood for a moment over the 'Mouth of Hell': a gouged cliff inlet where the sea beat with ferocious force at the face of the earth, contorting the very rock. Blasts of marine air forced open and then filled the mouths of the rare visitors to that peripheral terrain: every act of breathing entailed an involuntary saline swallowing. Alongside the Mouth of Hell, a trickle of disintegrating wooden stalls run by figures with morose, salt-encrusted faces sold shoddy trinkets to mark the end of Europe. Waste paper spiralled in the stormy ocean winds that perpetually assaulted that zone of clapboard squalor, forming an ultimate debris. The sky and the ocean were gaining ground, dismissing the last, blighted traces of humanity. Along the coast, at the Cabo da Roca, Europe at its western-most extreme faces out to the Atlantic. Immense cliffs rise deliriously over the sea, and the land mass of Europe forms a vast harshness that finally gives out, in elation, with a sudden fall.

To arrive back at your point of origin in Europe, to close the journey around its edges, requires obstinate determination. When the journey locks north, on its final stretch, the mind goes numb and aims, as though in panic or by caprice, to head in any other direction, to try to burst open a permanent sensory liberation in either the act of travel or the matter of Europe. And you discover that the points of departure and destination will no longer mesh in a seamless closure, since Europe has mutated out of joint in whatever interval has elapsed since you set out, the levels of time and space mismatched, pulled adrift both by Europe's ongoing transformations and by the raw exigencies of the journey. Its last

stretch, by far the most direct, is also the most torn.

Along the Atlantic face of northern Europe, the speed of the journey suddenly changes; the stuttering arhythmias of eastern and southern Europe have vanished, replaced by a stable but breakneck pace. That propulsion finally re-ignites the euphoria of the journey's initial stages, but this time, it is generated in the form of a visually contaminated variant. The railway lines follow alongside or cross over dense webs of motorways, their channels loaded beyond capacity and bordered by a near-continuous procession of vast retail parks, motels and supermarkets. The train shoots by before you have the chance to catch the corporate names on warehouse signs, but then, before any interval has passed, another conglomeration of exactly the same buildings succeeds the previous one. Still, the names elude you. The visual substance of north-western European cities remains intangible, strangely alien and unfamiliar, with nothing grasped or held in the eyes, until you find yourself gazing out into a hypnotic emptiness, caught in a sensory void of Europe. At night, the trains progress more erratically, with sudden ellipses of movement at junctions, and the journey through illuminated cities begins to file its way back into vision. To the eye of the traveller, the spectacle of north-western Europe is one of harsh recurrence, its visual zones maximally patrolled and replicated. In the rooms of corporate chain hotels, all of the televisions transmit the identical pornography channel and the walls breathe out the same sifted air. Around them, the visual screens of the cities relentlessly project a set of images whose repetition rapidly encompasses the eye and forms an integral part of the body, to your horror, in Europe.

At its end, the journey around the peripheries of Europe leaves behind only a scattered residue of sensory impressions and memories, all of them inevitably intertwined with the impact of the pervasive media screens and surfaces which intimately surround the course of any traversal of contemporary European cities. The images generated from those media screens relentlessly take the upper hand over the fragile substance of memory, until it becomes pounded down to a few blurred but tenacious shards. In the cities that border Europe, the great avenues appear ensnared within their own visual secretion, the inhabitants compelled – whatever their initial resistance or hesitation – to participate utterly in that culture. It literally does not matter whether those digital surfaces transmit consumer products, or desirable human forms, or technological innovations, or national obsessions: everything is ultimately sieved, as an undifferentiated pulp, into the eye. I wondered if there had come a point when the intricate languages of Europe had irretrievably fallen away from their cities and passed into dereliction, but – whether it happened long ago or just recently – the ascendancy of the image is transforming those archaic languages towards eventual extinction. In Europe, you inhabit the unreal seizure of immediacy that constitutes the present. Perception is engendered entirely from visual components, and the insistent hold of that visual culture is nowhere more pronounced than in Europe's border zones. The always-contrary periphery is cemented together by means of a visual emanation that possesses no matter, and whose crucial work is always to evanesce with spectacular power. Within the thrall of a journey around Europe, it becomes increasingly impossible to separate yourself from that visual envelopment, and equally impossible to judge it. In the end, the media cultures of Europe appear as a system of apertures, which open and close in tightly controlled sequences. They work to expel or shield whatever is needed or not needed in Europe at each moment, functioning as though oblivious to their own ephemeralness. And as you try to gaze outwards, beyond the edges of Europe, you are also forced simultaneously to look inwards, into the heart of its digital future.

On the margins of its cities, the sexual culture of Europe generates an intense transaction. In eastern Europe especially, the mass operation of prostitution – with the shipments of young bodies wholesale from poverty-stricken areas into the affluent western countries – forms a further link in those regions' repeated deportations and forced evacuations of populations, the trajectories of which defaced much of Europe's twentieth-century surface. It is as though the glowering eyes of Stalin now preside over the arctic, nomadic sex of prostitutional eastern Europe. All of the night boulevards of western European cities carry the over-exposed faces of young eastern Europeans whose lives have been cancelled out. The journey around Europe substantiates the myth that the very origin of Europe itself was stamped with an indelible sexual violation. But, at other moments, it appears that sex has almost been wiped off the corporeal map of Europe, transposed instead into the domain of media imageries and endless pornography websites. In the future, it may shrink away forever, detumescent and contaminated; from its first to its last digitalized exhalation and spasm, sex in Europe is a headlong rush into evaporation. In the subterranean sex clubs of Hamburg and Marseilles, with their punishing human imperatives, it seems that perhaps the deviant zones of Europe are where sex can survive, for the time being, in multiple amalgams of exacting intent and experimentation.

Europe's sexual culture is a vital presence, riotously smeared in contradiction over its undignified face. It leaks ecstasy. The single haunting image of European sex is that created by the sexless figures of the prostituted young exiles lined up around deserted late-night railway stations, their skinned-alive faces veiled by the glaring light emitted from advertising screens.

The peripheries of Europe are marked out by the violent traces of extreme political factions, with opposing aims, that clashed throughout the twentieth century. Strangely, a calm suspension or abandonment of those entrenched conflicts seemed to coincide with the new century's beginning. I wondered, at the end of my journey, if extremist political culture itself had finally vanished from Europe, or whether it had grown latent in more mainstream political power. Certainly, the fierce urban conflicts that I had sometimes encountered by accident a decade earlier – pitched battles in the suburban wastelands and marketplaces of decrepit eastern German cities, enacted with head-splitting wooden staves and metal bars by yelling neo-fascists and militant ecologists or young communists, leaving pools of blood in the dust and concrete – seemed to have disappeared. Everywhere, from Austria to France, it seemed that the extremist factions of previous decades had meshed, more or less cleanly, into more central political structures that were themselves too preoccupied with media strategies or financial corruption to know or care what was happening. When the extreme enters the centre, a conflagration is invariably in prospect. But, as I travelled, the peripheries of Europe appeared to have become too exhausted by the gruelling confrontations of the twentieth century to re-stage those rigorous conflicts, as though the restless urge towards extremity had finally suffered a numbing collapse in its sensory cortex. Even the vitriolic exclamations of competing neo-fascist and neo-communist graffiti, which had once been layered intensively over tenement façades, had now fallen into neglect. The young faces of the cities' inhabitants seemed diffused; it appeared that for any of them to subscribe to an extreme conviction would result in the too-painful cohering of an existence that required a random dispersal and distancing of its brutal elements to prove tolerable. The extremist edge of those cities had dissolved in the pulses of visual captivation. But such an appearance of terminal stupor is deceptive, and Europe's aberrant history remains deeply fissured with moments when an apparent state of coma in its political extremities became abruptly stimulated back into one of uproar.

On the peripheries, the senses are sharpened. Each moment when what seems to be a final edge to Europe is reached – the panorama from the castle above Butrinte, or the plunge of the eye into the Mouth of Hell in Lisbon, or the endless perspective from a flight over the Urals – brings with it a sensory clarity that makes its appearance only when a powerful entity has been induced to release its grip. The journey around Europe incites an integrally unsettling, even feverish experience, and that intermittent sense of lucidity marks an interval where the fever breaks before rapidly re-establishing itself. At such an interval, every intricate system of subjection or containment that constitutes Europe also appears to have been momentarily relinquished, leaving an empty space behind; that sudden release conveys a sensory revelation. All tangible, corporeal and visual traversals exact their own upheavals, and in Europe, such shocks to the sensorial order operate with maximum urgency within its extreme boundaries and metamorphosing zones. If the journey around the European peripheries were to be propelled onwards, indefinitely prolonged, it might eventually lead towards a fundamental corporeal transformation, attuned to the relentless demands of those peripheries and engendering a kind of 'extreme body' of contemporary Europe. But it is ultimately the eye that forms Europe, constricted within the visual spectacle of its cities' avenues and projected outwards to the points at which that overpowering compression is suspended and Europe opens out with all of its vital respiration.

Vanished Europe: Berlin from Century to Century

I made a journey across the edge of the European twentieth century, in Berlin, and came out at the other side, in a zone of disappearance. Berlin is an extreme in time, and every media voice that approached that temporal precipice was stridently demanding a moment of purification in which the atrocious historical entity of twentieth-century Europe would be expunged forever. This entity's great malediction – whose source, throughout the century, had been Berlin – would be removed. But out at the other side, at the start of the 21st century, Berlin's disquieting presence proved to be intensified, its human content erased, its visual-media power consolidated. Europe itself appeared nullified but surrounded by a gradually fading debris of virulent images that kept its periphery alive.

At the beginning of the 21st century, all media images and languages of Europe engage in a fierce struggle to claim the peripheries, undersides and limits of Europe, to annex its determining extremes in their visual, physical, mental, historical, philosophical, mythical and geographical dimensions in order to cancel them out. The media image has the overriding advantage in its impact of proprietorial banality on the entranced eye of Europe's inhabitants, and for any resistant language of Europe, only one aim remains: to interrogate the last traces of Europe's peripheral screen, the living, tenacious carapace of images that encloses its identity. Europe's interior identity is already void, transparent, and is filled by an aura of media hallucination, of promotional and commercial frenzy, of shards of nostalgia that comprise its mortified contemporary experience.

The exterior, extreme screen of Europe is diluting fast. Following the invention of photography and cinema, it aggressively ground its way into Europe's face, exacerbated its effect via the twentieth century's store of corrosive images, uniquely able to pierce vision and sensation. Now, the media of Europe are taking their revenge. Within a decade, this exterior screen may be gone, like a fragile ecosystem disintegrating in a cloud of pollution. For the present, viewed at the peripheries, it still formulates and projects the presence of Europe through imageries of its cities, human bodies, historical ruptures and implosions. Within that screen, the immediate imageries of contemporary Europe collide with the shattered and eroded imageries of its recent past. The intimate placing together of those disparate imageries generates a manifestation of Europe that is always in intensive confrontation and demanding interaction with any inhabitant who approaches it.

On the periphery of Europe, the experience of that revealing screen of images is both enticingly vivid and catastrophically unsettling: its acute precariousness makes it more and more volatile. It forms a beguiling apparition in the vision of the inhabitant of Europe, whose perception is transformed into that of a spectator who is either engulfed by the screen's emanations or incited into pursuing an interrogation of his or her place within Europe: as an exile, a migrant, a displaced individual, a resisting prisoner, an enemy, an expelled absentee, a complicit member, a captivated participant (experiencing the pure visual ecstasy of belonging) – or any permutation of those positions simultaneously.

Caught in suspension on the peripheries of Europe, its inhabitants are confronted by a visual babel, a cracked and collapsing wall corroded as much by its own unbearable content as by its gradual acquisition and enforced dismantling by Europe's contemporary media. Its images possess a visceral texture, tainted by the twentieth century's wounding of vision itself, that disorients and overhauls the sensory capacities of those inhabitants. The imageries of Europe are always transmitted vertically and upwards, in an architectural movement determined irrevocably by Albert Speer's design of 'cathedrals of light' for the early Nuremberg rallies; but the sensory impact of those imageries is directed horizontally and outwards, in a compulsive visual stream, with a relentless rhythm, towards its spectators, with an accumulating effect. After a time, out on the sensory peripheries of Europe, spectators' perception starts to habituate itself to that livid screen and can assimilate individual imageries and their combinations. These imageries of European cities proliferate and multiply in temporal tension with one another, with pixilated images of contemporary cities set against those cities captured at the pristine origin of the film image itself. These imageries project urban landscapes in mutation – images of cities reduced by disaster to scorched-earth terrains, cities impelled by mass celebrations or demonstrations, cities entirely overtaken by immense building projects. These imageries show Europe at the very heart of its transformations. Among the elements of that visual flood, human faces are perceived – images of great swarms of lost and subterranean human presences, of ecstatic and contorted mouths and eyes. On the peripheral screen of Europe, all of those pulsing images are transmitted simultaneously, crushed crudely together, layered into each other, colliding, merging, amassing.

At these peripheries of Europe, the sound experienced by its inhabitants is constituted from borderline discontinuities: it oscillates between silence and cacophonic over-audibility, backwards and forwards, grating across the limit between human noise and city noise. Driven into a capricious response by image and noise, the inhabitants of those visual borders can even dip a hand into the screen of images – so tangible is the visual scarring of Europe – and disrupt its flow, by focusing and isolating the projection of a particular image onto their bodies, from where it seeps indelibly into the internal terrain of memory to create their own instance of Europe. By this corporeal act, they also become aware of the incipient evanescence and fragility of the imageries at Europe's edge.

Within that peripheral screen, the existence and heart of Europe are visible but also possess an historical dimension for their spectators – a perception that is positioned in a state of salutary upheaval by the visual experience at the edge of Europe. Occasionally, from that vantage point, the unscreened interior identity of contemporary Europe becomes momentarily apparent, revealing a transparent, schematic terrain blunted by the oblivion exacted by its media into a desultory state of loss. Even the resilience of atrocity and its imageries will become a matter for nostalgia, in Europe's anaesthetic future. Europe's contemporary identity – timeless, its origin cancelled out – forms a central sensory black-out: its own end.

In the very last days of the twentieth century, I travelled through Berlin. I walked across the city, from the far west to the far east, through a terrain of transformation. I had somehow had the delusion that, since the city had determined Europe's crucial collapses and elations and had generated its seminal images, Berlin as an entity would come to an end at the same moment as the century did: dissolve into space as surely as so many other immense and powerful historical cities, such as Gortyn, had done. European cities established

53

in grandeur for thousands of years had abruptly disappeared without a trace, been abandoned into gradual invisibility or brutally layered under the constructions of other, disparate cities on the same sites, as in the case of Byzantium. Within the infinite timescale of Europe, Berlin's hold on the dirt of the Brandenburg plain formed a skewed claw mark, with the city's industrial expansion into vast tenement districts taking place only in the final three decades of the nineteenth century. Even Hitler and Speer, in their ever-proliferating architectural obsessions, had envisaged the complete disappearance of unruly Berlin and its supplanting by the imperial metropolis of Germania. In its brief existence, in fact, Berlin had literally disappeared once before, crushed to ashes, its human figures decimated or hidden, as film and photographs shot by the Soviet forces in the first week of May 1945 demonstrate with acute power. During the following decades, the regimes on either side of the division of Berlin had implemented an enforced screening-away of the other side, literally cancelling its existence on their mappings of the city, each using intricate strategies to impede the path of any aberrant vision on the part of its inhabitants. As though its contemporary form had accumulated as the tenuous residue of all of those planned or actual annulments, Berlin now seemed eminently ephemeral at the end of the wounded century it had inflicted upon Europe. All of the vast reconstruction work across eastern Berlin, together with the spatial seizure of Potsdamerplatz by corporate headquarters – the towers erected for Sony and Deutsche Bank – appeared as the manifestation of a wry endgame that Berlin was playing with Europe, taunting the century through to its final exhalation.

As I travelled across the face of Berlin, every avenue and visual perspective opened out into gaping multiple dimensions, magnetizing the eye, as though I was making a journey

54

around Europe's dizzying periphery once again. I knew from a thousand such journeys in Berlin that every movement taken through the city disintegrates intractably into shards of images and human figures. For once, though, I had chosen a fixed trajectory across the city and intended to follow it. I wanted, one final time, to pin Berlin down in my mind, like some spectacular butterfly species nearing extinction, before its moment of definitive vanishing.

Among the great houses of Charlottenburg, at Berlin's western edge, you walk in burnished light. Their inner courtyards collect the sounds from a hundred high-ceilinged rooms, magnify them to crystalline intensity and project them vertically into the air. In the northern working districts such as Wedding, the multiple series of back courtyards recede from the street, accumulating in squalor, decreasing in fresh air, until the farthest courtyard is the one where the scream of terror or noise of a factional or territorial murder reverberates, spinning down into the dirt between garbage containers and abandoned toys. Life itself is muffled and silenced there, never reaching the light. In Charlottenburg, the vast nineteenth-century houses were constructed so that affluent families could inhabit twenty or thirty rooms on one storey, around a single courtyard of pristine air. The corridors within filter out like a web of streets, and the polished wooden dining tables also stretch endlessly, far beneath the silver chandeliers.

The over-solid houses of Charlottenburg form a fragile terrain of ghosts. Their upper storeys were inhabited in the 1920s by artists and photographers, many subsequently exiled or exterminated, their studios requisitioned for Nazi families. By the early 1960s, the central boulevards of Charlottenburg had become showcases of the German 'economic miracle', their pavements lined with prostitutes and consumer display rooms, forming a bizarre counterpart to the austere splendour of the Stalinallee on the other side of the Wall. In the postwar decades, artists in West Berlin gathered instead in the Kreuzberg district of blackened, abandoned factories, declared their sense of nausea at the prospect of setting foot on the luminous Charlottenburg boulevards, compounded as that ground was of the oblivion of atrocity and an ensnaring substance of lust and greed.

The first step taken on a journey west to east across Berlin begins on such torn, deluxe ground, but projections of horror or distaste onto those blithe boulevards dissolve in the accumulation of other image projections – digital-image screens, vast advertising hoardings, department-store displays – that surround them as they reel in blank exhilaration. Around

Zoo station, where the Charlottenburg boulevards converge, the lost, detrital population of western Berlin seethes in determined self-cancellation, as though attempting to emulate the ranks of images that tower around them. All across Berlin, around its railway stations, those entangled amalgams of abject human bodies and digital images form nodes of collapse. Zoo station's entrance hall conveys its eminently human aura of sexual disease and alcoholic internal organs. At night, the far side of the station extends the crooked line of prostitution emanating from the Charlottenburg boulevards, with each desperate boy waiting for a cruising car to transport him to the demolition sites nearby. The exclamations gutturally crushed or spat out from these encounters possess the cadence of voices from the eastern edges of Europe, and the gutters glitter at night with the debris from shattered bottles of sweet red Crimean wine.

From Zoo station, crossing western Berlin, the atmosphere abruptly quietens, homogenizing into a silent swathe of apartment complexes constructed in the 1960s which emit only the slightest of pulses: an elderly widow out walking a dog, a scattering of children in a play area. The city bleaches out like an overexposed image, and its surface only buckles at rare intervals: at the bridge over the canal where the battered corpse of the murdered Rosa Luxemburg was thrown into the water in 1918, or at the Bendlerblock building where many of the participants of the failed 1944 coup against Hitler were executed. Over the twentieth century, one atrocity was nonchalantly exchanged for another in this city, just as one calm everyday silence mutated, passed through fire and emerged as banal as ever.

All of the buildings erected for business conglomerates in Potsdamerplatz carry a strange presumption. Somehow, these construction projects seem to be the results of a ludicrous naïvety. The buildings remained woefully unfinished at the end of the twentieth century – the inside of the Sony building, especially, looked grotesquely dishevelled, its spaces blocked with wooden spars and strewn concrete blocks, as though manifesting a derisory European sabotage of the pure streamlining which a building designed for a Japanese company should possess. Close to the location of Hitler's bunker, the viewing platforms arranged around the building site appeared to have been constructed specifically for looking downwards, in anticipation of a summary levelling, rather than upwards, towards the soaring towers. Down between those towers, a huge, messily gouged crater held back a rechannelled mass of water via an intricate arrangement of barriers and metal scaffolding; deep down, in that vast scoop of seeping dirt, hundreds of workmen scurried and slid about in concentrated activity, covered in thick red mud, yelling hellish invective at one another. It looked as if they were burrowing insanely into the ground, for no other reason than a mass obsessive compulsion, so making a valid, aberrant architectural response to the site.

In those last moments of the twentieth century, the Reichstag building gave out an insular, self-absorbed emanation: seared clean from its foundations to its newly transparent dome, it carried no statement other than its own accomplished expunging, projecting itself in sharp antithesis to the building whose cancelling images show it in flames in February 1933, and densely marked with exclamatory graffiti in May 1945 by the elated Soviet soldiers who captured it. A few years earlier, when it had still appeared mottled and jarred as though vulnerable, not yet recovered from multiply inflicted blows, this building had formed the vivid screen for the pre-eminent spectacle of Berlin's final twentieth-century years. In July 1995, its wrapping by Christo in vast pieces of grey fabric had emptied it of all power. Although Christo announced that he wanted the building to disappear momentarily, to create astonishment and nothing more, by night the wrapping precipitated a visual overhauling of the entirety of Berlin. The Reichstag became one of Europe's extreme screens. For several successive nights, in the summer darkness, great crowds gathered to sit in front of the building on expanses of grass that would be supplanted by building sites by the century's end. This population of spectators created its own cacophonic soundtrack to the existence of Berlin as they gazed in awe at the spectacle of nothing. The darkness transformed vision into individual intersecting trajectories of imagery and memory, and from that void surface, images from the past, present and future of Berlin were incessantly generated in a revelation of the city. But on the final night of the wrapping, the fabric had already started to come undone; cranes had been positioned around the building in preparation for the imminent removal of the unravelling screen. The last night's spectators were restless, silent. The unique screen was dismantled before its participants' eyes in a painful tearing of vision, and the murderously banal spectacle of everyday life in Berlin slid powerfully back into place, at least for another moment.

On Unter den Linden, a boulevard running directly west to east, the linear traversal of Berlin reaches a point of equilibrium. Even the surviving traces of the GDR – the pedestrian lights with their squat man in his wide-brimmed hat, striding at green – remained in an even distribution, ten years after that state's extinguishing, with the brutally eye-seizing system that had arrived to replace them. One set of traces subsisted precariously, with zero underpinning, while the other intractably gained territory, and the balanced visual textures of the boulevard veered erratically, from step to step, in one-sided combat. The eroding set of traces endured only at the far end of the boulevard, over the river Spree, in a square inhabited by glowering statues of Marx and Engels. The metallic screens surrounding those two delinquent figures still held stencilled images evoking revolutionary movements in Africa and South America: some remained undisturbed while others had been abruptly cancelled with wild 'X's. An image of Erich Honecker, the GDR's stultified leader in its final years, carried the most intent mark of negation. Honecker, a bizarre concoction of frozen autocrat and endearing buffoon, left deep wounds of nostalgia after his departure; in August 1991, at the time of the inept coup against Gorbachev, I heard isolated elderly voices in the tenement backstreets of eastern Berlin whisper, in fearful excitement, that Erich would surely be coming back, and now, he would be angry.

In the streets above the Spree, I walked by tenement houses that shone intensely with their recent renovations. Only a few erratic houses – whose ownership was disputed, or whose proprietors made a profession of lethargy – still maintained the level of pure disintegration which all of them had possessed a decade earlier. In the years after the fall of the Wall, when those streets had formed the axis for the city's experimental culture, entire roads of creaking houses had deteriorated to the extent that pedestrians had to keep an eye permanently turned upwards for the moment when a terminally crumbling façade or balcony would come crashing down: every month, at least one inhabitant of the area would be crushed into the pavement by such a collapse. This neglect was exacerbated by the impact of wartime damage in the enduring form of deep structural traumatization. Only the coagulation of five decades of engrained dust and dirt glued together the cracked matter of those streets, left to erode

60

since the moment when Soviet forces had stormed through them, leaving spattered blasts from grenade explosions and machine-gun fire around windows or cellar openings. All of the attention towards housing in the GDR had gone into the construction of satellite suburbs of raw concrete-block towers, far out on the eastern edge of the city. The centre rotted down, the dust-and-sunlight atmosphere entailing a gradual inhalation of those corroded houses. The interiors were no better: broken wooden floorboards, blocked heating ducts and waterpipes, and the aura of lin-gering fear seeping out from behind the resolutely locked doors of older residents. The streets flared into life only in the nightclubs and gallery spaces created in the back court-yards, in derelict factory spaces, often subterranean, where the production of materials vital to the survival of the GDR – shoddy cement, brittle plastic – had suddenly been arrested. Through every night and dawn, the pavement of Auguststrasse convulsed with the cardiac techno-music uproar beneath it. Inside the nightclubs, between bouts of frenzied dancing, the peripheral young inhabitants, drawn from every country of Europe and beyond, watched con-densed steam from their soaked, overheated bodies drip from the roof tiles; outside, at the end of the night, the breathless air of the frozen winter streets splintered their wet hair into icicles.

At the end of the decade that had seen those streets erupt – in a multilingual concoction of elated young voices, with bodies forever tearing up and down the pavements in great waves in the dead of night – they had once again grown somnolent. The voices had been erased, in the same way that the last traces of the 1920s advertising hoardings, painted directly onto the façades in an indelible medium of tea and still vivid 70 years later, had all been chiselled away or layered over in brash colour. Inside, the apartments now possessed what had been inconceivable luxuries a decade earlier: telephone lines, hot water and baths, in addition to the digital luxuries that had yet to be conceived when those defunct houses were emitting the sonic signals of their imminent ruination. Almost all of the art spaces which had hosted interrogations of the human body's borders in a transformed Europe had closed, lying dormant in anticipation of their eventual mutation into shopping complexes. As I walked from end to end of mute Auguststrasse, a group of property speculators was standing in the centre of the street, briefing clients on how the walls between minuscule apartments could be removed in order to produce more valuable spaces. Only the ice in the air remained from the street's blazing moment of resuscitation.

From the revolving summit of the Television Tower, three hundred metres above Alexanderplatz, at the heart of Berlin, I looked down over the city and traced the line of my journey. In defiance of my desire to make a linear movement directly across Berlin, the city's terrain appeared to have imposed the shape of a zigzag traversal onto my steps: a line contorting in places, blunted into dead-end reversals in others. Any line through Berlin is cut; as a strategy for survival, the city simultaneously engenders in its inhabitants the need to complete what is broken in its substance and to mesmerize perception into oblivion with the conviction that nothing was ever really cut. The only movement that remains inviolable is an ascent away from that scorched ground such as that which brings the eyes into gaping contact with the entirety of Berlin from far above it. Like the movement around the peripheries of Europe, the horizontal traversal of Berlin is in acute spatial flux, at once impossibly condensed and opened: a journey that transforms the eye until it can itself create the city.

Along with Zoo station, Alexanderplatz forms another of the fractured axis points that punctuate the path of Berlin's overhead-railway line in its own traversal of the city. Around Alexanderplatz, with its minute details of human destitution, vast digital-image screens tower over the concrete steppe; the images and the empty surfaces are intractably locked together, each possessing its own annulled, cold majesty. A tentative population makes expeditions across the Alexanderplatz, their points of destination opaque, hidden from view by obsolete hotels and department stores from the GDR era that still clog the space like massive glacial deposits. Even without those obstructions, human vision would reel blindly here; the only exits are the pedestrian-subway open-

ings at each far corner, leading obstinately to uncrossable road junctions and to further subways. But after leaving Alexanderplatz, the contortions imposed on every journey through Berlin abruptly fade away, with an ultimate perversity, and the final part of the crossing of the city takes the form of a soaring escape along the undeviating expanse of Karl-Marx-Allee.

I walked the entire length of the boulevard, with darkness falling, held within its glowering splendour. All through the previous decade, the exterior walls of the Karl-Marx-Allee apartment buildings had attracted an intricate layering of graffiti that had metamorphosed in inflection from year to year, fluidly crossing sexual, political and emotional ground. Now, this graffiti had been obliterated. When the boulevard had been constructed, at the beginning of the 1950s, as Stalinallee, the builders had rioted in the face of their exploitation (the sumptuous apartments, unique in that ravaged part of the city for their luxury, were destined for party bureaucrats) and had been viciously crushed, thus infusing East Berlin with the originating tension that ran throughout the existence of the GDR, eventually overriding it in November 1989. The entirety of Karl-Marx-Allee had now been handed over to a company of property speculators. At the far end of the boulevard, at the point where the city's eastern customs gate had once stood, a tiny shop sold exotic fish for aquariums. On the façade of the shop, an archaic sign dating from the 1950s showed a contented, open-mouthed fish exhaling three fabulous bubbles of green neon. Beyond that point, the infinitely replicated concrete blocks stretched out eastwards: the last breath of life had leaked out of Berlin.

I walked south, at the last moment of my journey, down to the Oberbaum bridge across the river Spree; the tenement district of Kreuzberg extended on the other side. Whenever I travelled to West Berlin during the years when the Wall still stood, I would come to this point on the river's edge at nightfall, at the moment when the city's flocks of birds wheeled overhead, soaring and falling in intricate floods of movement; the river itself marked the then-lethal division between the two Berlins. A great laceration seemed to press down on the city, its power most acutely exposed at that point. The nineteenth-century bridge was used as one of the heavily guarded crossing points between the two parts of the city: barbed-wired, blackened, war-damaged, it appeared ferocious – an isolated shard of the city, saturated with the history of Europe. Now, the bridge was open, renovated to immaculate splendour. Night had fallen; I walked halfway across the bridge and looked back along the black river. I could feel the laceration still there.

At the end of every journey across Berlin, an accelerated reverse movement abruptly sends its linear intentions into vertiginous freefall. My journey doubled back on itself, east to west, like the moment in Alexander Medvedkin's 1938 film *New Moscow* when the projector screening a film of the young architects' opulent plans for Stalin's rebuilt capital suddenly jams and goes haywire, and the images of the city speed backwards in time, from their contemporary grandeur to their ludicrous origins in atrocity, or ashes, or dirt. In its unravelling, the journey reveals itself and all of its seminal images, but with such rapidity that the eye has to go into overdrive to seize even one or two of those images. And then, before I knew it, the twentieth-century city of Berlin was gone.

From the aeroplane window, the expanse of the Brandenburg plain is finally cut by lakes and forests; the plane starts to descend, and the first tentative houses appear, then arrangements of tenement streets, factories, towers, the Spree, and the plane descends into the city. At that point, as it touched down, I was at last convinced that I had experienced only an obstinate delusion in believing that the expiry of the Berlin of the twentieth century also somehow entailed the entire disappearance of Berlin itself; when I returned in the spring of 2000, the city was still there, still pulsing with images. Down on solid ground, I could feel that something had changed in the life of the city.

From the other side of the world, I had watched the media images of the end of Berlin's twentieth century: the celebrations and fireworks launched in arid spectacle around the Brandenburg Gate. Barriered and steaming crowds, studded with politicians, watched the explosions in the sky. The last night of the year in Berlin was always a cacophonic furore, with hundreds of windows shattered by firecrackers unleashed to expel the hovering demons of the old year and repel the incoming demons of the new one; for the first time, that yearly riot of expurgation took place under a rigorous control. The media images of Berlin had jarred against the other images of celebrating European cities: every accompanying word spoken about Berlin was inflected with a sense of relief, as though the integral power to damage which that city held, and transfused to Europe, had now been mercifully drained away, returned to zero.

As I attempted to follow my journey of a few months earlier, it seemed that even the air of Berlin had lost its cohesive tension. On the Charlottenburg boulevards, storms of cherry-blossom petals, whipped by turbulent hot air, swept around pedestrians, impacting weightlessly on their faces. The intentionality of the city had snapped. My steps veered off waywardly in every direction, my eyes constantly drawn away at tangents; I followed only the media images of the city, and the journey I had made in the last moment of the twentieth century proved to be irreproducible. It appeared that Berlin had been invisibly transformed as it passed through that moment, with the placing of an enveloping skin of infinitesimal volume over all of its abysses, extending to cover its entire surface; above the great squares, that skin mutated, intensifying into the form of digital-image screens. And from that pacifying skin, all of the sensory compulsions of the city now emanated, in endless repetition, void before their projection had begun.

Even over the span of a few months, the suturing of Berlin had taken greater hold. On Unter den Linden, the precarious balance I had earlier gauged between the surviving traces of the GDR's imageries and the growing onrush of banal consumer imageries had now been skewed, and the idiosyncratic evidence of that bizarre regime had been almost entirely obliterated. The Potsdamerplatz corporate towers, still incomplete, appeared more secure on their foundations, while out on the edge of Karl-Marx-Allee, the neon fish that had exhaled its gulps of fluorescent green ether into the Berlin night was now boarded over. Berlin's digital homogeneity had become capable of melting any resistance or aberrance on the part of its inhabitants with instant ease. The spaces of the city were now held under tighter surveillance, visually tracked and relentlessly appropriated. Even in the GDR, with its grandiose apparatus of gazing – millions of citizens watching and documenting the behaviour of others, in perhaps the most sophisticated voyeuristic system the world has ever known – the labyrinthine arrangement of Berlin still provided innumerable hidden spaces. Now, the seamless visual surveillance of the city was being executed without human flaws, without even any intention to chastise its recalcitrant citizens, since none remained; the city's consensual capitulation to its engulfing media thrall had erased all of the desires and imageries that had compulsively enlivened it over the previous four decades.

The fractured, deeply layered terrain of Berlin had vanished, replaced by an anaesthetic, transparent media skin that, in its banality, formed an inverse surface to Christo's intricately sensitized screen over the Reichstag, where the volatile imagery, memory and history of Berlin had uniquely coalesced for an instant. But it seemed inconceivable that the memory of the city had dissolved so completely. I decided to explore some of the peripheries of Berlin, at points where its historical shattering was irreparable, still resonant, to try to discover at least one or two images or sites where a revealing provocation to the eye and memory could still hold its ground.

Looking for the surviving elements of Berlin, I walked through the sunlit streets of the eastern Karlshorst district. In the years before and immediately after the fall of the Wall, those streets had been the exclusive preserve of the Russian military; at the far end of Rheinsteinstrasse, the concrete villa in which the German surrender had taken place, on 8 May 1945, had housed the Museum of the Unconditional Capitulation of Fascist Germany in the Great Patriotic War. At a moment when it seemed that all of the authentic, deranged elements of memory and time in Berlin had themselves capitulated and been driven into outer-space oblivion by the city's contemporary media surface, I imagined that this could be a zone in which a few stray traces of those

elements might remain tangible. It was exactly the 55th anniversary of the surrender. The Russian forces were long gone, their ceremony of departure in 1994 marked by a manic dance performance by the inebriated Boris Yeltsin which managed to encapsulate the magisterial lunacy constantly projected by the Russian presence in Berlin. Only a few grey metal shells of sentry posts now remained, scattered along the streets, their exteriors rusted, interiors gutted, concrete floors diamanté-d by long-broken glass.

The original museum, which had exalted the mission of the Soviet army in the destruction of Berlin, had been supplanted in the mid-1990s by a new museum ostensibly dedicated to promoting friendship between Russia and Germany. But strangely, the content remained almost unchanged from the last time I had been there, nearly a decade earlier: the creaking rooms were still filled with the same vast panoramas of the storming of the Reichstag, and the soundtracks from film images of partisan executions and Soviet military advances still resonated around the space, projected from video monitors. The postwar images of Russia tailed off in the mid-1980s, and no presence emerged from the incoherent matter of contemporary Russia to permit a sense of empathy with Germany to gel; in the implacably locked imagery of Russia, only digital images of the bombardment of Chechnyan cities could seamlessly replace the monochrome celluloid images from 1945. Around the exhibition rooms, gangs of visiting ten-year-old Berlin schoolchildren ran wild in aggrieved elation at their momentary liberation from school and confinement, their voices pulsing into dismissive hysteria whenever their restless eyes caught sight of images of massacres. Every institutional site that marks out mass killings by means of loaded imageries, from the firebombed or A-bombed cities of Japan to the concentration camps of Germany and Poland, engenders an identical response of abrupt repudiation in resistant young eyes, which realize that they are being emotionally triggered and coerced into the grip of a concentrational media system to which they are not yet entirely habituated.

The space of Berlin had come unstuck at that moment in Karlshorst, existing in chaotic limbo between the city's present and determining but repudiated past. In the gardens around the villa, aged Soviet veterans nostalgically inspected the preserved tanks that had taken part in the decimation of Berlin, while inside the building, competing sounds of taunting young laughter and outraged official voices tore the space apart. Finally, the schoolteachers had to bundle their sullen children out, and only the sounds of exploding shells and soaring warplane engines remained.

The chandeliered room in which the capitulation took place had been used as a German military casino in the prewar years. One side of the space, with its enormously high ceiling and windows looking out onto the villa's gardens, still held the long, baize-covered tables around which the delegates from the victorious factions had sat as the surrender took place, while a digital projection screen had been anchored to the ceiling above the other half of the room. Far above the eyes of its spectators, that screen showed the surviving film images of the capitulation: jump-cut images, shot in tremulous hand-held movements by war cameramen evidently still shaken by the events of the preceding weeks. The soundtrack accompanying the silent images leaked in from the gardens, through the open windows: elderly Russian voices in the foreground, against the constant sound-mesh of the contemporary city. In those images, the greatcoated participants of the surrender landed at Tempelhof airfield and were driven rapidly through ruined streets towards Karlshorst.

The film cameras swept over the devastation during that seminal traversal of the city. Almost no human figures were visible among the levelled buildings: only one or two stiff-limbed people stood by the roadside, momentarily captivated by the sight of the speeding motorcade. The participants reached Rheinsteinstrasse, arrived at the villa and strode into the room in which the images were now being projected. The German military commander, Keitel, read the surrender document with evident repugnance, signed it and was taken away, while Stalin's commander, Zhukov, initiated a drinking session that continued until the images suddenly cut; the screen went blank for a time before starting the ten-minute sequence again. The two parts of the divided room cast their disparate evidence into the space: the side of the room where the signature took place mutely emanated its amassing of memory, while the side dominated by its image screen unendingly repeated that headlong silent journey across the shattered terrain of Berlin. Once again, the Karlshorst space emanated a strange sense of limbo. The two halves of the room existed in tense flux: the static atmosphere of one side summarily overruled by the compelling power of images, which in their turn were subjugated by the definitive presence of memory.

Later, in the museum's cinema, I watched films of Berlin's destruction, projected to mark its anniversary: the Soviet soldiers reached the north-eastern suburbs of the city, still fighting step-by-step under explosions of flame in the skies; then, after finally taking the Reichstag, their scarred faces moved from frozen intensity to exhilaration as they embraced in celebration. They crowded around the battered walls and columns of the building to inscribe upon it the marks of their hard-won presence. A few rare images had also been shot by the encircled Berlin inhabitants in those days: terrified and exhausted families hid in cellars, anticipating an imminent carnage of retribution; then, in the days after the fighting had stopped, bundled figures on dog-carts scavenged desperately for food. The films' spectators watched the images in shock, exclaiming out loud – even though many of them had experienced the events themselves, such images now rarely reached the media channels of Berlin, and they reactivated memory in vivid bursts. The images had been collected, in the final years of the GDR, by a now-aged and shunned documentary filmmaker, Karl Gass, who saw them as images exiled from the contemporary surface of Berlin, only able to reach that surface at points where it momentarily broke down. In the contradictory existence of the city, nothing could be simultaneously more archaic and so essential to Berlin than those images.

Back out on Rheinsteinstrasse, all of the images evanesced instantly in the city's retrieval of its inhabitants' perception. In the fading evening light, girls in black dresses stood at the Karlshorst tram stop, heading for parties, and children played in the spaces between the apartment blocks constructed for the vanished Soviet forces.

Europe was divided up in 1945 like raw meat, sliced arbitrarily, each jagged territorial cut executed with nonchalance. Whatever devious strategies or underhand manoeuvres had impelled the sets of cutting hands, in attempting to allocate countries or populations to particular systems, their rationale was overturned so rapidly by Europe's spontaneous contortions that only the spectacular gestures of power exuded by those cuts remained. In the postwar decades, Europe was infused by the lack of purpose in its division, with immense floods of human figures displaced and channelled into one regime or another – totalitarian, democratic, socialist – as though by an opaque mishap from which any trace of an encompassing vision had instantly leaked away. In eastern Europe, only the brutal consolidation of those originating gestures of power held that mishap together and gave it bogus substance; the visual emanation of eastern Europe proliferated out from that cold core, in a rash of endless concrete cities and terrains of acid pollution inhabited by subjugated figures. Four decades or so later, Europe was finally ready to contort again, seismically shaking its eastern regimes away like obsolete debris.

At the Cecilienhof, on the south-western edge of Berlin, Stalin, Churchill and Truman met for the Potsdam Conference to perform their gestures of power two months after the Karlshorst capitulation. The film and photographic images of the division of Europe carry the vital indignity held by its future. In those images, the three participants appear distracted, hardly there at all. The great striding exits and entrances of the Karlshorst images are absent. Stalin laughs derisively with his aides as if he was about to allocate tractors to Ukrainian collective farms for the hundred-thousandth time. Churchill, who would go missing in mid-meeting, appears lost and dumbfounded. Truman conveys an ebullient, desperate self-consolidation, as if he has somehow found himself exiled to a rural insane asylum with two particularly deranged room-mates. On the terrace of the Cecilienhof, with the Jungfernsee beside them, the three proprietors of Europe sit in uneasy proximity; only Stalin appears at all aware of the film cameras and photographers, subjecting them to withering oblivion.

I made a journey to the Cecilienhof, at the base of the narrow, forested lakes that run vertically along the western edge of Berlin, dividing the city from the Brandenburg plain like a long set of gorgeous scars. In that expanse of water-land, constellated by Hohenzollern imperial palaces in disparate styles, by huge parks and follies, the tenement concentrations of central Berlin seemed far away. After the respiratory intake of that landscape, however, the corrosive urban buildings would resume in the swathes of GDR-era apartment blocks spreading out across Potsdam. I crossed the blackened Glienicker Bridge, where the Cold War exchanges of prisoners between the two German states had been staged, and entered the parkland that lay between two stretches of water: the grey Jungfernsee, whipped by winds, and the tranquil Heiligersee, around which groups of naked sunbathers lay spreadeagled in the hot air. Until 1989, the banks of the Jungfernsee had marked the division between the GDR and West Berlin, with the Cecilienhof positioned only a few steps inside the Wall. Over the tree-covered isthmus, where the temperature suddenly cooled, the Cecilienhof appeared in its bizarre splendour: the last of the palaces to have been constructed in that landscape, it formed a leaden approximate imitation of a Tudor mansion of a kind seen only in the suburbs of Tokyo.

Inside the Cecilienhof, the rooms appeared stultified, frozen at the exact moment when the meetings of 1945 had ended. Part of the palace had been closed off and converted into a luxury hotel, but I walked through the rooms that had been assigned to each of the meetings' participants, to the central hall where the desultory haggling over the future division of Europe had taken place. The owners of the palace had then only recently fled, fearing that their support for Hitler would render them prime candidates for Stalin's wrath. The Soviet forces had organized the meetings, and of the three participants, Stalin had received by far the superior room, luxuriantly red-carpeted and spacious, its windows

looking out over the lake. Churchill's wood-panelled room, by contrast, appeared cramped and shoddy. Although the central hall had been damaged by a neo-fascist arson attack a decade earlier, it appeared pristine in its preservation of the surface detail of the meetings, with flags indicating the participants' places at the round wooden table.

From Stalin's window, I looked out over the banks of the Jungfernsee. The Cecilienhof emanated an attempt to enact a purification of atrocity, to convert the burnt-earth zones of Europe into perfect segments and to fabricate a capricious Eden from mounds of incinerated bodies. In defiance of the meticulously preserved interiors of the palace, all that had survived from that futile work of the summer of 1945 was the sense of a deep fracture in time and space, through which the contemporary moment of Berlin poured in, mocking that pre-eminent pretension to impose a design on Europe. In that building, Stalin, Churchill and Truman had aimed to engender a delimitation of Europe, but Europe resists the imposition of such boundaries, forever creating and transforming its own parameters. And the crucial mismatch between the ambitions enacted in the Cecilienhof and the contemporary surface of Europe revealed Europe's capacity to divest itself effortlessly of whatever powers or imageries might be imposed on it. No images are secure in Europe: all of its powerful media screens could be cast away as abruptly as the future that was formulated in that lakeside palace. The time and space of Europe move in intricate sequences of contradiction and reversal; the ultimate revelation would be to discover what lay behind – and after – its annulled media screens.

Back on the avenues of eastern Berlin, I made one final journey to try to discover an element of the city that had not yet dissolved into homogeneity. It seemed that only the collisions between the contemporary city and those pivotal sites that had launched Berlin's postwar trajectory from ruins held the capacity to expose its future form. Alone, those sites and monuments appeared entirely moribund, vanishing into obsolescence, just as the digital-image culture of contemporary Berlin possessed no existence beyond its instantly extinguished projections. But held together, in volatile amalgams of memory, image and history, those two contrary elements made the city's deep, extreme contours materialize.

I crossed the Spree to Treptower Park. The morning traffic moved at speed down the road that divided the park's two sides. Opening out from an archway indented into the overlapping trees along the road, a broad path led through to the Soviet War Memorial. Along the path, the squat statue of a

grieving Mother Russia initiated the emotional searing that the memorial was intended to exact from its spectators. The viewer's eyes then had to sweep abruptly over to one side to reach the focus of that emotion: the immense figure of a Soviet soldier towering over the treeline at the far end of the memorial terrain. In one arm, he held a rescued child, while a concertina'd stone swastika was crushed beneath his boot. This figure stood on a massive, conical burial mound, incised by a steep flight of steps; inside the base of the statue, a gated crypt was surrounded by a wall of mosaics showing a group of mourning Soviet citizens. Bordering the vast avenue that held the ashes of soldiers killed during the final assault on Berlin in April 1945, a sequence of stone friezes carried images of the conflict, ascending on either side towards the statue of the soldier, in elliptical bursts of condensed narrative, each image anchored at its base by a block of declaratory text, in

gilt lettering, attributed to Stalin; one sequence of images carried their text in German, the other in Russian. The memorial had been built over the second half of the 1940s. The architects had deployed a punitive irony in their materials: the figure of the soldier had been constructed with marble from Hitler's Chancellery, and the viewing area for spectators had been assembled from the stores of granite brought to Berlin in anticipation of the victory monuments to be erected in Speer's triumphant new city of Germania.

For me, the Treptower Park memorial formed the very origin of memory in Berlin: I had seen it on the first evening I ever spent there, in 1979, at the age of seventeen, ten years before the Wall had come down. At that moment, the memorial site had appeared almost as a city in its own right, possessing its own unique system of space and time: it was located close to the Wall, placed between the restless Kreuzberg district of West Berlin, with its narcotic nightclub culture, and the dream-locked south-eastern suburbs of East Berlin, where the silence of the deserted streets was only occasionally interrupted by the spluttered backfiring of Trabants. The memorial encompassed its transient population, drawn from the eastern European countries, who traversed its expanse with awed concentration. They studied Stalin's inscribed pronouncements intently and stared at the narrative sequence of war images as though at an epic film of long, fixed shots which imposed its own decelerating timeframe in order to saturate its spectator's gaze with its entire contents. Every few minutes, another huge group of wide-eyed Bulgarian factory officials would arrive in a ramshackle tour bus, all wearing identical grey suits or dresses of over-ironed polyester and following an imperious guide carrying their national flag. Anyone who lagged behind for a moment would receive a cutting reprimand. The spectacle appeared outlandish but compelling, and I followed at a distance behind one group of corralled visitors, then switched to another, unable to understand the languages they spoke but somehow captivated by the sense of being a western European anonymously splintered into that intense, alien visual engagement.

After the Wall came down, it rapidly transpired that I had been mistaken in imagining that any sense of authenticity could be attached to those devoted gazes, assembled under the pressure of fear rather than through engagement. The hordes of eastern European visitors diminished abruptly, and the site was neglected, kept together in its original grandeur only because it could not be demolished. The texts of Stalin were spray-canned into illegibility for a time – their gilt lettering was lost forever – and the only visitors to the site were inhabitants of nearby Kreuzberg in search of a gratuitous moment of hallucination or a view of the collapse of empire; they nonchalantly scanned the memorial's stone images as though assimilating a film being projected in excess of its habitual speed. For most of the inhabitants of East Berlin, for whom the memorial's overbearing impact had always hit too close to the bone, the site simply vanished from the face of the city.

In the last moment of the twentieth century, I visited the memorial in the dead of night. Voices yelled invective at one another in the woods around the site, and I could hear the cries of an alcohol-fired sexual act from somewhere between the trees. As I stood beneath the burial mound, the figure of the Soviet soldier formed a massive, glowering presence in the dark, occasionally illuminated for a second by the headlights of a veering car being driven through the adjoining park on some drunken mission; otherwise, it remained deeply submerged against the freezing night sky. At that moment, I had the terrifying sensation of inhabiting a darkened space

"DIE IN UNSEREM
LANDE VERANKERTE
IDEOLOGIE DER
GLEICHBERECHTIGUNG
ALLER RASSEN
UND NATIONEN
DIE IDEOLOGIE DER
VÖLKERFREUNDSCHAFT
HAT DEN VOLLEN SIEG
ÜBER DIE
HITLERFASCHISTISCHE
IDEOLOGIE
DES BESTIALISCHEN
NATIONALISMUS
UND RASSENHASSES
ERRUNGEN."
J. STALIN.

in Europe possessed by vastly powerful, invisible presences. It was as though that space had suffered a sudden loss of consciousness; the act of awakening from that black-out would demand a transformed vision.

In the new century, I looked out over the memorial from the granite viewing area. A few figures were dotted around the site, walking in the sunlight or sitting on the steps cut into the burial mound. The numbers of visitors had risen in the preceding years, along with the city's expanding Russian population, and for the young inhabitants of eastern Berlin left undamaged by the GDR or Soviet occupation, this was a site of astonishment. The sequence of stone images along the avenue appeared finally to have found its equilibrium in time and space. The site was habitually denuded, but for a moment, to mark the anniversary of the fall of Berlin, a vivid mass of red roses had been placed against the body of the statue.

From the eastern edge of Berlin, in the most cracked and benumbed of the endless concrete-block city-satellites, you take the overground train that crosses the entire city from east to west. Soon, the housing blocks and supermarket complexes are left behind, as the train picks up speed and moves through the zones of wasteland that divide the central districts of the city from those peripheral human enclosures. Huge chemical gas-pipes appear from nowhere, inscribed in fluorescent graffiti, and run alongside the line. The train comes to a stop at stations where nobody gets on or off. Gradually, the eastern tenements of the city start to exert their grip on the eye, initially in tenuous clusters remaining from streets that have mostly been destroyed, then growing into larger masses. Around the lines, blackened, derelict factories are interspersed with prefabricated warehouse complexes, and to the north, the domed towers that mark the eastern edge of Karl-Marx-Allee emerge above the tenement roofs. The river Spree appears as the train rises above ground level and moves sinuously through the city's central areas, crossing repeatedly from one side of the river to the other. All of the city's eastern avenues converge around the vast plain of Alexanderplatz; up above them, digital screens and illuminated advertising boards relentlessly transmit their homogeneous, void imagery into the arena of the city. The train disgorges one population into Alexanderplatz and instantly acquires another. Bizarre miniature figures of Marx and Engels appear in the far distance as the train approaches the northern tip of Museum Island and crosses via an indentation in the buildings, where the remains of machine-gun fire from the time of Berlin's fall punctuate spray-canned graffiti exclamations. After the train passes through Friedrichstrasse station, a gouged terrain of immense demolition or building sites accumulates on either side of the line. The flawed visual texture of the city oscillates between its immaculate contemporary surface and its sudden collapses into decrepitude or damage.

The train crosses the river again, and the Reichstag makes its momentary apparition, almost lost behind the construction sites of corporate towers. For a few minutes, the evidence of the city disappears completely to one side of the train, the line edged by a swathe of parkland and canals, and the raging visual momentum of the journey slows down to a sparse, disjointed heartbeat; then, the hold of the city corrects itself as the train nears the virulent concentration of Zoo station. Most of the passengers exit, dissolving into the aimless, stalled crowds that coagulate around the station entrance. Once the train is released from that bitter seizure, the great avenues and houses of Charlottenburg immediately surround the line, and it is tightly channelled through that lavish space. Apartment interiors flash split-second images of figures in high-ceilinged rooms – embracing, fighting, staring back – towards the watching eye. At its western edge, the city gradually gives ground, tapering away in filaments of elegant houses. The train abruptly abandons its sinuous contortions as it exits the city, veering to the south-west and crossing tracts of thick forest in a straight line, until the journey is finally arrested alongside the Wannsee. The memory seethes with the images collected over the journey: in the span of an hour or so, you have traversed Berlin.

Simultaneously, as you stand on one of the city's fractured sites, where all of its levels of time, image and memory are compulsively divulged, the eye makes its journey through Berlin in an instant, and that unique traversal carries its own excavation into the matter of Europe. In Berlin, at the heart of Europe, you are also at the extremes of Europe: the city is an emanation of all of its wrenched components, of layers of human skin and building surfaces and digital screens and voids that intersect combatively, inhabited by torn figures that are both overwhelmed and energized by the presence of Europe deep in their arteries and eyes.

Occasionally, aberrant images of the human body form abrupt sensory eruptions and momentary bursts of contradiction in their movements across the face of the city, then just as rapidly burn out. And across Europe, day and night, those movements are replicated. Europe's rhythm pulses from those visual movements, and from the swarms of human figures that incessantly cross its cities at speed. All about them, a sealing, assimilating coherence is constructed around those cities' restlessly shifting, wounded façades, so that everything gels smoothly and falls into place.

But then, when you step back from Europe, or find yourself snared into its darkness, or when you reach its extreme peripheries, you find that all of the controlling surfaces that encase Europe are nothing at all, and can themselves vanish without a trace. The capacity to definitively erase them belongs exclusively to a power that does not form part of those visual empires, and cannot be accessed via their media screens. Europe is infinitely somewhere else.

European Breakdown Zones: Paris Suburbia

I made a journey into a zone in flux where the European past and future collide. The exit from Paris is marked by an infernal sensory cacophony and by immense advertising hoardings, secured to the roofs of corporate towers or apartment complexes and illuminated at night, far above the edge of the city. An unbroken stream of cars and trucks moves around that spherical border at every hour of the day and night. The six-lane motorway that encircles the inner city districts of Paris is called the Périphérique: the peripheral road. Once you have crossed it, from the interior to the exterior, nothing at all remains of Paris.

I spent a year wandering through the strange areas on the far side of that peripheral road, and I saw the vivid traces left by the lost twentieth century in a visual debris of broken images, in exiled eyes and voices and in outbursts of violence. In that non-city of non-citizens beyond Paris, the origins of the new century emerged from the crucial meltdown of those traces into a fierce human culture, visible in all of its seminal and transforming fury, over the edge of the city. That culture possesses the capacity to finally annul the powers that control and consolidate the peripheries of Europe, and to throw that rigidly patrolled ground of surveillance – and everything that lies within it – open to the wind. In the breakdown zones of Europe, outside the visual reach of the city, every image and act appears as if caught between the two extreme points in the history of Europe: the origins of liberty and the origins of restriction, censorship and massacre. The future of Europe and its populations remains poised in tension between these two contrary obsessions.

The areas beyond the city form multiple terrains of exile. The first floods of exiles from the conflicts of the twentieth century arrived to inhabit the far edge of Paris at the turn of the 1920s, in the wake of the Russian Revolution. The affluent exiles remained in the centre of the city, inflecting its roar with their language at the same moment that the avenues of Berlin were absorbing their own sudden mutation of populations and noise. An accompanying influx of destitute Russian exiles headed for the exterior of Paris, expelled from its centre by their poverty, unable to afford anything more than dank, peeling rooms in the decayed alleyways of outlying districts. Those alleyways had been constructed to accommodate the overflow of impoverished manual workers who were then forced to walk for miles at dawn, in great human torrents, to their workplaces in the central areas of Paris. But for the Russian exiles in suburban poverty, Paris itself barely existed in either of its guises – as a gorgeous city of luxury or as a city of gruelling sweatshops – and they remained preserved for decades in a hallucinatory limbo of nostalgia, holding on to a few rescued sepia photographs of their elapsed lives, unnerved into stasis by their memories of revolutionary massacres.

During the same decade, hordes of bewildered figures also arrived from many of the other eastern European countries, in one of the pulses of the great twentieth-century migration from eastern to western Europe, impelled by motives of survival and the flight from oppression, or by the need to generate income through manual work, prostitution or extortion. In the 1920s, especially, a large component of Polish exiles arrived at the city's periphery, to compensate for the shortage of manual labourers after the carnage of the First World War. The suburbs also increasingly swallowed an influx of gauche figures from the far rural margins of France itself, figures intent on an urban reinvention of their rigidly constrained lives. Paris was always primarily a destination of immigration rather than a launching site for emigration. Almost every other major European city lost swathes of its population, over the nineteenth and twentieth centuries, to immigration or colonial ambition, but the population of Paris remained tenaciously rooted. Even at the fall of the city to German forces in 1940, the initial mass exodus had been largely reversed within a few months, its inhabitants seeping back into the silenced city.

After the war, another population arrived in the suburbs to live alongside the remnants of the moribund community of Russian exiles and other uprooted elements. Workers came from North Africa in the 1950s to make a living for their families, left behind in their villages; after the Algerian war, at the beginning of the 1960s, they were joined by many thousands more who had allied themselves with the defeated colonial French forces and were not welcome in liberated Algeria. These populations inhabited cities of plywood and tin shacks built in the dusty wastelands – 'zones', as they were called – between the desolate suburbs, out beyond the northern and western edges of Paris. The 'tin-can towns' of shacks were doubly located nowhere, at the peripheries of the periphery. A cooking fire would often burn out of control in one shack, and the whole flammable city would immediately become engulfed. The cramped populations lived under tight surveillance and were vulnerable to violence and even mass killings by the brutal French police, as happened in October 1961 during a suppressed demonstration against the Algerian war. They formed another dispossessed human component of the suburbs, haunted by massacres and nostalgia, sustained only by tattered photographic images and memories of Kabyle mountain villages. The last of the plywood camps eventually disappeared at the end of the 1970s, and over the following decades those populations, with their families, were relocated to godforsaken concrete-block satellites in the same areas, where they were maintained in utter destitution and jammed into conflict with exiles from other countries. Throughout the 1990s, the new peripheral city-satellites often exploded in violence, becoming surrounded by overturned, flaming cars and charging riot police.

The Balkan and eastern European warfare at the end of the twentieth century sent a further population of exiles to those borderline areas, into housing compounded from cracked 1970s concrete and crumbling, sodden alleyways built in the previous century. A sudden influx of Yugoslavian manual workers had already arrived in the suburbs after the Second World War. But unlike that population and the peripheries' North African exiles – who worked long factory shifts or undertook the menial maintenance of the city centre – the eastern European refugee population of the 1990s was not expected to take on any activity and remained fixed in mental space like the Russian exiles of 80 years earlier, their memories of expulsion and horror initially too livid for them to perceive the landscape into which they had been dispatched. Eventually, they gathered to sit in small, mute groups around the concrete-block satellites or on benches in the suburban squares, their gazes oscillating abrasively inwards and outwards as they faced a return to their scorched-earth homelands or a clandestine life hiding ever deeper in the lost periphery of the city.

All of those populations – and many more, too: exiles from other former colonial possessions of France, and musicians and artists uprooted by desire or necessity from the prohibitive city centre – inhabited an unyielding terrain, over which a fine sensory debris of cancelled memories and blanching images gradually amassed. The concrete surfaces blared with vast graffiti exclamations, while the decayed façades of older buildings formed too delicate a screen to withstand those strident declarations of desperation and anger. Corporate centres and business parks filled many of the wastelands left by the emptied plywood cities, accumulating over decades as counterparts to the masses of concrete-block housing complexes. Offshoots from the peripheral motorway cut great furrows through the suburbs, and the inhabitants of that circular zone inhaled a corrosive, polluted air. At night, in the distance, the great digital-image screens and advertising hoardings above the peripheral road faced resolutely away from them, directed into the centre of the city.

But over time, the voices, memories and images of those scrambled, marginal populations started to reassemble themselves, from silence and oblivion, as though recovering after a stunning blow, and they began to imagine their own vision for the future of Europe.

Out to the west of the peripheral road, the corporate towers of La Défense crowd together beyond the edge of the city. They house no population, and at night, the wind whips through the immense Grande Arche that forms the central void among the towers, sending cartons and wrappers discarded during the day spiralling up from the empty concrete plaza below. Each of those minuscule, insane storms of debris and dust constitutes a mirage of aberration far below the pristine digital screens marking the summits of towers and department stores. This vast desert is a suitable point from which to begin a circuit of the city's periphery.

Walking through the constellation of towers late at night, the only human traces I found were lolling security guards in marble-clad entrance halls, their eyes rolling in exhaustion. The very act of opening your eyes in La Défense involves

gulping down over-illuminated images and surfaces. Behind
their image screens, the towers project themselves in a glowering, static choreography. In the utopian visions of Paris of a
century ago, it was envisaged that the entire face of the city
would soon become covered with such towers, in a vertigi-
nously bristling arrangement for which the Eiffel Tower was
intended to set an average height. Any surviving low-level
building would become an archaic perversion in that visionary
city of perpetual demolition and re-erection. But, contrary to
all architectural expectation, the city remained obstinately
set at low level – virtually untouched by the conflicts of the
twentieth century – and so the corporate towers and buildings
of La Défense had to be constructed at a distance from the
city centre, as though some dubious, unsavoury experiment
were being conducted behind a sanitary cordon. The first
building, the CNIT complex, completed in 1958, proved to

be a monstrous, mutant innovation, with its vaulted concrete roof – the largest ever constructed, designed to rival medieval cathedrals in splendour – cracking rapidly into decrepitude. The overbearing public sculptures placed on the plaza outside the CNIT were soon graffiti'd into submission. From the end of the 1980s, however, the groups of streamlined towers began to acquire a fraternal homogeneity, and at night, they form the sole beacon of the entire peripheral zone. The darkness annuls their ostensible corporate purpose, and, lacking spectators, their ludicrous commercial images transform themselves into vivid digital torrents drained of content. The towers emanate a mutinous blaze of taunting light directed towards the flat city lying below them on the far side of its peripheral road.

I walked behind the Grande Arche towards the long pier of wood and steel that extends outwards, away from the city, as though in headlong flight from that malign presence. In its original design, the pier was intended to project itself on and on, in gratuitous abandon, through a scarred terrain of motorway junctions and apartment blocks, to be cut only by the path of the Seine. But the end of the twentieth century marked the abrupt extinguishing of all such gestural aspiration in Europe, and the pier was abandoned after a few hundred yards, suddenly terminating its trajectory over a huge cemetery. The only inhabitants of the pier – spaced unevenly along its length and sitting balanced on both edges – were pairs of illicit young lovers from the adjoining peripheral areas, tightly moulded into one another in lustful oblivion of the beneficent towers that sheltered them from familial or racial prohibitions. At the far end of the pier, I turned back to the vision of the Grande Arche and its surrounding buildings, spectacularly tensed in isolation against the night sky.

The homes of the pier's lovers were only a few harsh steps away. The apartment-block towers of Les Fontenelles rose up as a bizarre apparition of tin-can shapes alongside La Défense, as though resonating with the 'tin-can towns' of North African workers that had previously occupied the area. From the pier, those towers had appeared almost as a down-beat annex to the streamlined corporate towers of La Défense, but approaching them, I saw that their alliance was tied to a far more lacerated terrain. Their shoddy façades were tiled in a garish camouflage pattern, as though the buildings' disappearance had been envisaged even at the moment of their conception. In the gaps between the six or seven psychotic tin cans of the Cité Picasso, their young population teemed in a restless, all-night frenzy of screamed, techno-backed insults and laughter, occasionally interrupted by yelled rebukes from insomniac residents leaning out in futile fury from the porthole windows indented into their buildings.

If some omniscient eye were to look down from the cloudless night sky onto the intimately adjoining areas of Les Fontenelles and La Défense, it would glimpse two peripheral architectural nodes existing in parallel universes: a raggedly concocted swathe of human uproar and destitution placed directly alongside a deserted but luxuriantly radiating arena of light. Between the two, the borderline remains mercifully permeable during the night to the sexual desire of the tin cans' young escapees; otherwise, it is invisibly but emphatically sealed.

On a journey on foot around the city's perimeter, the roads double back or give out, and you are soon lost. Blocks of luxurious apartments and shops appear in the distance, then disappear abruptly as you turn a blind corner and find yourself in a vast, abandoned expanse of broken glass and graffiti, between two suburbs which barely possess names. All around, motorway overpasses traverse the edges of the city in a fierce, relentless medium of noise. Once they have left the peripheral road behind, those highways divide and subdivide into a dense swirl of elevated channels, as though the logical fulfilment of their endless proliferation would be the transformation of the city's border zone into one great open highway, moving without transition into and out of it. The overpasses pinion Paris's terrains of expulsion as though exerting a cursory stranglehold, their heavy concrete limbs descending from far above the crumbling alleyways.

Beyond the city's north-western edge, in the district of Gennevilliers, the inhabitants live within the shadow cast by the overpasses. The dust and fuel residue that sinks down from the traffic lanes lies heavily on these figures as they make

their own arbitrary traversals of eroded neighbourhoods. The archaic blue-enamel signs in shop windows advertise products that no longer exist. Stray lorries thunder through the intermediate areas that divide those streets from the motorway slip-roads, their oil-sodden drivers stopping in front of two-storey shacks that house canteens downstairs and hollow-eyed eastern European prostitutes upstairs. The inhabitants of that lost suburb, drawn from every torn country in the world, possess haunted eyes. Only the presence of the river looping around their domain infuses a sense of freedom or escape, mythic in its intensity, into those eyes.

I took an empty road that followed, at ground level, the line of the concrete supports of an elevated motorway from the huddled streets of Gennevilliers out towards the river. Soon, the last exhalation of the suburb had given out, and the road began to run along a narrow peninsula between derelict quaysides. Directly beneath the motorway, a few children played in dirt and pools of rusted water; wheelless caravans on the quaysides contained abject figures for whom even a cramped tenement apartment formed an impossible dream. Cans and wrappers were jettisoned from cars on the motorway overhead and fell in an intermittent hail. Dogs ran in harried zigzags over that spit of land, with the detritus of the city down below and the speeding traffic up above. Suddenly, the empty road turned at a right angle, away from the path of the teeming highway, which then crossed the river and disappeared into a hillside. The final stretch of the peninsula road bordered the river on one side and the inlet of an abandoned port on the other, with the ruined traces of obsolete loading bays and crane supports still scarred into the quayside. It finally tapered out in a stone promontory almost entirely surrounded by water. I sat on the very end of the promontory with the cold river rushing by at my fingertips.

A barge came into view, passing below the motorway bridge, heading away from the centre of Paris. It ploughed its way down the middle of the river, painted an immaculate deep blue and covered with fresh flowers, the water behind it spreading out, in an intricate arrangement of ripples, towards the two banks. I could see the family on board, the father intently steering, the mother and two children engaged in some kind of 'I-Spy' game. That image of the nomadic, water-borne family froze in my eyes, and from my position on the extreme edge of the city, it seemed for a moment as though they were miraculously suspended in their flight.

On the eastern path of a circuit through the city's northern peripheries, the Stade de France is always prominently visible, appearing in omnipresent splendour above the low line of factory warehouses and decrepit apartment blocks. At the time of its construction, the stadium formed a strange puncture in the city's border terrain, as though its sleek form had been situated there by an inexplicable mishap. The very concept of building a stadium had a loaded history for Paris, since in 1942 the Jewish residents of the occupied city had been rounded up in a cycling stadium prior to their mass deportation. Designed for the 1998 World Cup, the new stadium had the ostensible aim of enlivening the morose surrounding streets of the Saint-Denis suburb. But the event illuminated those streets only momentarily, like the eye-searing radiation flash of an A-bomb; then its traces evanesced completely from the dour, ashen alleyways and dilapidated shopping complexes. On the evening of the football final, I flew from Helsinki into Paris-Roissy airport, out beyond the northern suburban ring of the city, arriving in Saint-Denis just as the spectators began to surge through the streets, in a tangible wave of exhilaration, towards the stadium. The entire city was possessed by a unique sense of elation, and, for one night, the intricate zonal arrangements of Paris's periphery dispersed in white-light ecstasy. In the hot summer darkness, after France's victory, all of the inhabitants poured irrepressibly into the city centre, conglomerating in a mass of millions of transparent figures, all divisions negated. The next morning, the stratification of the city re-asserted itself, though set permanently awry by the vast sensory upheaval it had undergone. The life-size cardboard figure of Zinedine Zidane appeared in the entrance of every supermarket, and the faces of the other players saturated the city's media screens.

Two years later, after the last-moment victory of France in the Euro 2000 tournament, the endless streams of peripheral figures descended from the suburbs into the city's central boulevards once again, but on that occasion, the celebrations misfired. The city's inhabitants attempted to replicate the exhilaration of the previous triumph, but the football final had this time taken place in a stadium in another country, rather than in Saint-Denis, and the uproar possessed no balanced focal points of departure and destination between the suburbs and the city centre. The surging population spanned the city, and the celebrations finally wheeled out of control, with some of the marginal suburban inhabitants unnerved or rendered furious by their dislocation into the city's hostile heart. By the exhausted end of the night, after confrontations between those phantom, stranded presences and the familiar riot police, the deserted avenues were laced with broken glass. But on the following day, in broad sunlight, the beatific presence of Zidane, beaming from a balcony above Place de la Concorde, erased the mayhem of the night.

As I walked across the addled plain of Saint-Denis, between the entangled channels of motorways and railway lines, I saw that the empty stadium had found its place in the zonal land-scape as a gratuitous addition to the sequence of immense, aberrant presences interspersed around the periphery. On its western side, the dominant presence is the glowering form of the Mont Valérien fort, where many Resistance fighters were taken to be tortured and executed, in secrecy, during the Occupation. That mass of grey military stone, poised in frozen malignancy above the city, still resonates with the infliction of a profound gash on perception. The stadium and the fort form deeply antithetical presences within the city's border – of ecstasy and horror – but their positions are allied: the determining extreme acts and emotions of the city become rapidly drained from its centre, their impact too provocative to be contained there. Instead, they are arrayed around the perimeter, in isolation from one another, pulsing incessantly between memory and oblivion.

The suburb of Aubervilliers, on the north-eastern edge of Paris, is compacted from that same material: in the early decades of the twentieth century, this was the sole suburb infused by the media of Paris with a soft-focus aura of affection and allure, and that collective emotional memory endured for decades, before it was engulfed in the 1960s by the evidence of harsh concrete and destitution. Aubervilliers is now a forgotten terrain within the span of the periphery's oblivion.

The invention of Aubervilliers as a mythic suburb occurred through images. In Elie Lotar's 1945 documentary film *Aubervilliers*, grinning children swim contentedly in the sun-drenched canal that traverses their suburb. The film's commentary depicts collapsing courtyards and their upright inhabitants, invoking the resilience with which they hold on to their poverty. For the film's intended viewers in the city centre, the suburb of Aubervilliers – only four miles to the north – was infinitely far away, and the heroism attached by the film to its inhabitants formed an exotic, idiosyncratic trait, as enticingly bizarre as the behaviour of France's colonial subjects as it was presented by the media of the same time. On a journey through the contemporary northern margins of Paris, it sometimes seems that the human contents of the former French colonies have been intentionally transposed to the concrete periphery for ease of usage and control, their populations enmeshed with the aim of pacification. But such a strategy of power has the potential to backfire ferociously by creating vitally insurgent cultures that annul the homogeneous media images generated in the centre of the city.

Even in the documentary films from earlier decades that intended to denounce the poverty of the border areas of Paris, such as Georges Lacombe's *La Zone* of 1928, their population is irresistibly projected as the charming denizens of an exotic, impenetrable land. They appear as ingenious scavengers, able to scrape a basic survival from the detritus and rags of the city centre, inventing endless uses for obsolete consumer products and selling them in raucous street markets. Their momentary incursions into the city to forage for these products occur before dawn; they vanish before its inhabitants awake. Their suburb is a magnetic terrain of lust where every commercial transaction is accompanied by a rapid sexual act. Occasionally in these films, former celebrities of the city centre are tracked down in that outlandish terrain, including a notorious cabaret dancer whose alcoholic plummet has led to expulsion to the suburbs to live in a caravan, but that fall is taken nonchalantly, and the dancer performs blithely for the film. The suburban alleys stretch out in those bleached images from 80 years ago, the pavements walked by huddled, stooped figures in black and by groups of wild-eyed children.

The traces of the ramshackle old courtyards seen in the 1945 film images of Aubervilliers subsist intermittently between the newer concrete towers, and the canal – the only highway visible in the film – survives as a battered, graffiti'd conduit for the ejection of the city's waste. The houses surrounding those courtyards appear to be in permanent suspended animation – their dereliction intact in mid-collapse – though more densely packed with inhabitants than ever. But the fabulous media aura of Aubervilliers as a beguilingly flawed paradise vanished at the same time as France's colonial power began to mutate. In the streets, the most evident new landmark is the mental hospital that houses those inhabitants for whom the lucid insanity of life in the suburbs is finally not sustainable.

Farther out from the peripheral road, north-east of Auber-villiers, the edges of the city possess no decayed residue upon which to layer themselves, and the vast satellites of 1970s concrete blocks expand unstoppably, attaining spectacular dimensions. Their architects at some point evidently grew weary of infinite replication and envisaged either blocks that contorted in intricate spirals or huge towers – such as those that form the main satellite of La Courneuve – that came complete with their own square void, indented midway down each tower, through which the wind could tear. At night, in La Courneuve, the core of life, inhabited by its overwhelmingly young population, is the bare community hall used for *raï* concerts and glaring eye-to-eye encounters. Outside the hall, under acetylene streetlights, the police presence is heavy, every machine gun-toting, black-clad figure scanning the crowds for an infringement of the rigorous prohibitions that govern that extreme zone. Every lost existence there is edged by nervous fury and by a consuming nostalgia that, without any surviving images to sustain it, forms a violent sensory wound.

In the suburb of Bobigny, even further out, the atmosphere becomes less fiercely charged despite the identical landscape of endless concrete apartment blocks, catatonic commercial centres and gangs of glaring boys clad in leisurewear. The tension between city and suburb diffuses completely; the population could be inhabiting any peripheral site on any continent. The inhabitants are so trapped in their lassitude that no exterior effort to oversee or visually direct their acts is necessary any longer, and the buildings' raw grey walls possess no texts, not even any of the image screens that are omnipresent elsewhere. Only a few tattered supermarket posters littered around the central plazas reassure the inhabitants that they belong to a civilization. In that visual vacuum, no will to engender their own images compels them. Paris and Europe have ended; the inhabitants' blurred eyes seem to dream away in detached, restless movements.

On the southern trajectory down the edge of Paris, after that dreaming abyss, the extreme proximity of the city and its expelled zones reasserts itself with a brutal jolt. The peripheral road comes into view again, though now it is often embedded in the city's face, running through underpasses and cuts rather than soaring overhead on concrete legs. Its path remains emphatically marked out by immense screens that, at night, tower over the road, illuminating its subterranean presence in lividly incandescent letters or symbols and in digital images transmitting short sequences in homage to particular media conglomerates. The vehicles below speed on, seeming to circuit the city but never arriving, propelling their cacophony over either side of the road.

The suburb of Montreuil begins with a sprawling street market of intense activity. The peripheral road is deeply incised into the ground at that point, its lanes stretching out within sheer walls; the market stalls extend along its far edge in a frenzy of tentative transactions in which almost nothing is finally exchanged. Midway over the bridge that borders the city and the suburbs, the first vendors stand their ground in the miasma of fumes issuing from the vehicles below. They desperately clutch whatever potentially saleable debris they have accumulated from their wrecked lives: a single shoe; a broken transistor radio whose speaker was fisted-in in fury, decades ago; a butcher's skinning knife. The hundreds of stalls abruptly spread out in a swathe of stolen goods, minuscule electrical circuits, nails of all sizes and already-worn eastern European suits. For a few weeks in the summer, the temperature rises enough for small boys to sell soda cans from buckets, barking again and again the revered names 'Coca-Cola, Sprite, Orangina', but for the rest of the year the exposed market terrain remains isolated and frozen, traversed by iced winds of dust channelled by the road. The destitute clientele is deeply cautious, forever moving from stall to stall, warily gauging minute price differences, and any sale forms a rare event generating elated hand-pumping celebration between vendor and client.

A perpetually sustained outburst of noise rises from the vendors' vocal tracts and hovers over the stalls in a dense, stormy cloud. Over the course of a year of passing through the market on my journeys around the city's perimeter, I heard the language of those voices switch, again and again, from North African to Polish to Russian. The displayed products changed abruptly, too, with myriad piles of shoddy, unlabelled t-shirts from Polish sweatshops jettisoned in favour of blue-hooped sailors' jerseys illicitly filtered across Europe from Russian naval warehouses. The inhabitants of Montreuil fingered each successive batch of items gingerly, with narrowed eyes and shaking heads. In the alleyway café beside the market, a giant bearded seller of Tunisian origin told me that the market had become lethal, with eastern European mafia gangs invading it, driving away many of the original vendors, but then discovering to their horror that the market generated precious little wealth. My preferred moment to pass through was always dusk, when the aluminium poles of the stalls were being disassembled for the night, and the homesick vendors gathered over vodka to bemoan the bad luck of that day, of the day they'd been born, and, most of all, of that cursed zone of Montreuil. Eventually, the eastern European gangs gave up and evanesced towards another peripheral pitch, and the market's wayward rhythm of chanting North African voices reasserted itself.

Over the expanse of Montreuil, the subsiding old alley-ways and factory buildings degenerated impassively, as though they possessed all the time in the world to achieve ultimate disintegration; many of the derelict, bare-brick factory spaces had been taken over by artists and turned into vast studios. In spite of the suburb's chaotic maze of alleyways exuding deprivation, its inhabitants strode around purposefully. During the decades when most of the adjacent suburbs had become defaced with rashes of concrete apartment towers, Montreuil had been under the control of a communist mayor who preferred, in contrary autonomy, to channel funds allocated for urban regeneration into the construction of a complex of GDR-style civic buildings, which now lay boarded up behind a high wooden carapace in the suburb's centre awaiting demolition. The memory of that mayor – visible in archival film of Stalin's funeral, at the lying-in-state, weeping inconsolably beside the body, itself as poker-faced as ever – had survived, his name having mutated into that of the Montreuil bus station.

On the eastern extremity of the suburb, over gentle slopes, great terrains of peach trees had been cultivated from the seventeenth century onwards; production had finally halted in the 1950s, though almost nothing had been built since then on the now-vacant lands. Sections of the orchards' ochre sandstone-block walls still stood, enclosing wastelands where occasional clumps of aerosol-inhaling, leisurewear-clad figures lay spreadeagled on the fertile soil. I walked over these empty fields. The huts of the peach farmers and the thick-walled warehouses once used to store harvested fruit stood abandoned, but the air still somehow smelled sweet, as though the tang of the pressed juice had so saturated the atmosphere, over centuries, that it remained indelibly present.

In Charenton, at the south-eastern edge of the peripheral road, the eye reels at the gaping perspectives, as though the city had been abruptly slit open with a butcher's skinning knife, its undersides spilling into vision. The river is disgorged from the city at that point, along with vast tracts of multiplying railway lines like those which mark the eastern exit from Berlin. From the bridge over the railway lines, high-speed trains can be seen every few minutes, roaring up on the last stretch of their journey from the hot cities of the Mediterranean coast. The Rhône valley from the region of Marseilles forms the pre-eminent conduit of transformation for Paris and its suburbs, with populations, images and voices collecting at its base and then coursing up like a scorching geyser that finally hisses out into the open air, its impact spreading vividly over the dour, moribund streets.

But behind that rapidly coursed zone of railway lines, in the old communal courtyards of Charenton, the population appears subterranean and immobile. It forms the most acutely exiled and melancholy of all of the city's expelled elements, comprising an extreme mixture of young and aged inhabitants who still cling to the edge of a city which has proved unyieldingly too expensive or high-powered for their discarded lives. The cobbled, shuttered courtyards, silent and airless, form trapped internal cities of muffled sensory echoes. They only revive sonically at night, in outbursts of fierce domestic altercation or when populations of somnolent cats discern fish among the evening's jumbled cooking fumes and stream across the cobbles from every window, yowling and converging on the source of the odours.

In the vast wooded parkland surrounding the seventeenth-century buildings of the Charenton asylum, whose most notorious inmate, 200 years previously, had been the Marquis de Sade, I came across an abandoned outdoor cinema hidden among the trees. Everything was intact: the projection box, the tightly packed rows of wooden benches and the metal screen. The projection box was even inscribed with the date of the cinema's construction: 1951. It had been built during the rare moment of experiment and openness in French psychiatry that had succeeded the administrative brutality of the Occupation, during which a strategy of starvation for asylum inmates had been pursued and their mass deportation to concentration camps planned. During warm summer nights in subsequent decades, the asylum nurses must have led the excited or catatonic inmates out over the park, in single file, and sat them down, in silence or crying, under the pine trees and the stars, to absorb the glittering images thrown by insect-shrouded beams of white light. From the quantity of rust coating the metal surfaces and the thick vegetation growing between the cracks in the benches, it looked like the cinema had been abandoned for at least ten years. At some point, the asylum doctors must have decided that the inmates no longer required the stimulus of images to enliven their drugged eyes in the darkness and that monotonous television transmissions – in some whitewashed room reeking of carbolic acid – would be the perfect medium with which to terminally blur and dull their senses. That corroded screen was the sole inoperative image screen in the entire city periphery, and the only one capable of resuscitating lost vision.

At the confluence of the Seine and Marne rivers, close to the railway lines that traverse Charenton, a huge concrete pagoda, the 'Chinagora', juts out far above the grey water that churns around that sharp junction. Passengers on the high-speed trains arriving from Mediterranean cities must believe that they are suffering sudden hallucinations when they glance to one side, from the bridge crossing the Marne, and momentarily catch sight of that strange apparition: they are not arriving in Paris after all, but in a glowering city compacted from image shards that can sometimes fly out of control on the suburbs' slithering surface to astonish or damage the eye. From the balconies of the restaurants and markets inside the multi-storey Chinagora complex, the panorama across the filthy water is soon annulled by the walls of derelict factories and docksides on the far bank. Inside the market halls, full of round vats of cooking oil and lurid landscape tapestries, Chinese voices sustain themselves in permanent interrogation, a world away from the volatile vocal rhythms of Montreuil. The pagoda lies at the tip of a tapering peninsula otherwise occupied by low-slung shacks and sleazy bars inhabited by disabused men and bewildered Ukrainian sex-refugees. But the presence of the two rivers somehow serves to bear those buildings and their peripheral inhabitants up, as if in flight, as if transporting them on a soaring journey beyond the city's suffocating range. Like the mythic land of antiquity between the Euphrates and Tigris rivers, this precarious terrain seems uniquely capable of human transfiguration.

Downriver from Charenton, the suburban satellites that inflamed the northern perimeter of the city appear again, encompassing its southern edge in a wide arc of concrete scars, intermittently cut by industrial zones and vast commercial centres, and made to adhere by violence and oblivion. In Créteil, in the far south-eastern corner, the salubrious tiers of apartment complexes, arranged around one side of a wind-swept artificial lake, generate a rare aura of deeply ordered calm flickering between the comatose and the void. Most of the inhabitants of those salubrious blocks work in the adjoining government buildings which tower in severe splendour above the lake. But behind the lakeside buildings and the commercial centre that bluntly substantiates them, cramped ranks of identical apartment blocks stretch out along empty roads, traversed only by occasional isolated figures carrying empty plastic bags and dreaming of mountain landscapes in Armenia, of anything other than the walls rising around them. Like the blank façades of Bobigny ten miles due north, the surfaces of Créteil carry only an erasure for the eye, which turns inwards or directly into the path of whatever deadening images it can find. On the constrictive strips of grass between each block, gangs of children gather to affront one another at dusk; up above, the blue glare of television sets illuminates every room.

Across the river to the west, the suburban arc continues in Vitry, where the 1960s blocks stand in an intricate geometric pattern of intersecting curves and lines, as though intended by their architects to be read from above as a hieroglyphic exclamation, or else conceived by the same unearthly eyes that designed the convoluted crop circles in the fields around Avebury in southern England. Even viewed from ground level, from the surrounding slopes, Vitry seems enigmatically charged, a result of its participation in the great illusory myth of the suburbs. For the original inhabitants of Vitry, the myth that sustained their lives was that of communism; many writers and artists moved from the city to those concrete megaliths in the late 1960s, at the time when the centre of Paris was detonating into street riots and the idea of a rigidly communal existence seemed the only way forward. The beckoning figures of Mao and Ho Chi-minh and the ineradicable face of Stalin must have flashed compulsively before these inhabitants' feverishly dreaming eyes like glowing deities. But by the early 1970s, the isolation of the Vitry blocks had begun to drain the mythic dimension from these stranded lives, and the

113

factional followers of Mao and Stalin spat vitriol at one another in their corridors like back-biting dogs. Gradually, the twenty-storey buildings emptied out their riven idealistic elements, and exiles from the peripheries of Europe and ex-colonial Africa and Asia moved into bare apartments with views towards the distant city. By the end of the twentieth century, a finger-jabbing media frenzy around the 'crimes of communism' – with the calculated millions of dead placed directly alongside those of fascism – had driven the last remnants of Vitry's original population into guilty self-oblivion and invisibility, their spectacular myth finally reduced to ashes.

As I approached the blocks of Vitry, the intricate design they had possessed from a distance abruptly evanesced. The visual flood of familiar, homogeneous destitution blithely layered itself over the obsolete ambitions that had initiated that suburb. A vibrant cacophony formed of seven or eight meshed languages blared from the open windows of each graffiti-screened building. Every morning and evening, the inhabitants of the blocks face a long walk to and from the distant suburban railway station, to take packed, dirt-encrusted trains into the city, pressed eye to eye, to undertake sweat-shop or street-gutter work. Their journey is the contemporary form of a regulated entry which has evolved and mutated ever since the division between the city and its impover-ished suburbs was instituted, but this journey has always possessed an identical sequence of movements over the span of a day: an abrupt mass entry, a tolerated interval of manual work, then an equally rushed exit. That endlessly repeated journey into and out of the city was executed on foot in the 1920s by workers from eastern Europe who emerged and amassed from their alleyways in relatively close proximity to the Paris boundaries; it is now experienced via crammed commuter trains from the ever-further-expelled peripheries.

The children of Vitry, cursing, shouldered one another aside, their eyes seized within a brutal hypnotism of corporate fast food and leisurewear brand-names. The trail of concrete satellites moved on relentlessly across the southern perimeter of the city.

Around the south-western edge of the peripheral road, the river loops its way out from the city at the opposite corner to Charenton. The desolate zone of sex shacks and eye-impacting incongruities that marks the river's south-eastern exit is an unknown landscape for this disparate extreme of the city. The salubrious headquarters of the city's media conglomerates and television stations border one bank of the river, sunlight shimmering off the reflecting glass walls of their multi-storeyed façades. Each opaque media tower is surmounted by a vast digital screen that transmits the same magnified images that are simultaneously being emitted by fifteen million or more television sets around the city and its suburbs. The polluted sky over those towers gulps the void images down. At night, far above the knotted highways, the illuminated signs on the roofs of the media towers imprint their corporate names against the darkness in vast letters, signalling their undisputed ownership of the city.

The suburbs that twist around the far bank of the river abruptly become wealthy at that point, as though the city's periphery had finally become fatigued by its endless concrete-block squalor and desired a capricious aberration to punctuate the last stretch of its frayed circuit. The land rises and falls as though in elation at that perverse trick inflicted on the city's morose face, and over the vertiginous terrain of the suburb of Meudon, luxurious villas ascend and descend in a contagious aura of vagary mixed with lassitude. From

their high altitude, the villas' elderly inhabitants look out in weary distaste from the padlocked gates of their gardens at the vast panorama of the city below, as it boils down in a medium of noxious traffic fumes and overheated images. Despite the city's visual proximity – made more immediate by the elevated dominance of the suburbs – it remains a world closed away.

Every silver-spooned boy and girl lost in the suburbs yearns to escape their stasis and surreptitiously embrace the city sprawl, no matter what the cost or disgrace may be of their flight from luxury. But towards the bottom of the river valley, the wealth of the suburbs peters out completely, and only a few decrepit eighteenth-century villas sustain a semblance of tenuous grandeur. From that low elevation, the city blurs into a flat white disc, arhythmically pulsing. In the 1950s, the infamous novelist Louis-Ferdinand Céline – author of *Journey to the End of the Night* – inhabited a crumbling villa in that peripheral terrain beside the river, between the suburbs and the city. Whereas the inhabitants of Vitry would choose, in the following decade, to exit the city for the suburbs as an attempted realization of their dreams of communism, Céline became an expulsed, endangered presence at the city's edge, reviled for his fascist affiliations of the prewar years. Only that marginal, blanched-out zone allowed him the space to disappear.

Adrift in the centre of the river, the Île Séguin contained the archaic ruins of the Renault car factory, abandoned when production accelerated to the point that the island could no longer sustain it. Every last scrap of space had been engulfed by the factory building, which still resonated with the memory of the vanished decades when the suburbs had been the domain of impoverished but fiercely militant manual workers. Between the fissures in the graffiti'd walls, rusted remains of the production lines were visible, severe figures of wrenched metal. Beaten into obsolescence, the dead weight of the factory island formed a monument of malediction conjured up to curse the digital industries that had nonchalantly superseded it and the city that had cast it away.

Through the vacuum of the western suburbs, the roar of the adjacent peripheral road resounds in turbulent echoes; the road, hidden discreetly in its raw channel from those salubrious streets, still emanates its grating disquiet. The towers of La Défense rise up in the distance: the journey around the extreme circuit of the city is reaching its terminal point. The bare sensory tremor of the suburban streets suddenly gives out, and the wooded expanse of the Bois de Boulogne blocks the way. No lucid traversal of that terrain is conceivable: at night, the woods are violently barriered by the cries of wildly rampaging gangs and disciplined acts of prostitution, with bodies tearing hot-breathed through the undergrowth in desperate flight; by day, the endless marshy paths appear more opaque still, sending you on ever more intricate dead-end circuits through tree-darkened spaces. Then, when you least expect it, the labyrinthine grip of the woods propels you abruptly out onto a wide gravel path that leads directly into the final suburb.

Caught between the insanely blazing towers of La Défense and the blunted drone of the peripheral road, the suburb of Neuilly lies embedded deeply within itself, wrapped in a chrysalis-pure state of never-emerging transformation, respiring its own silent, siphoned atmosphere. Any wounded memory of the city's concrete-block peripheries seems a blatant hallucination in Neuilly's great tree-lined avenues of mansions, private clinics and schools, from which emerge crocodile-files of elaborately uniformed children, holding hands as they cross the empty, patrolled roads. Even the affluent villas of Meudon appear crassly ostentatious in their gaping exposure to the city when compared to the insulated nineteenth-century mansions of Neuilly, each tightly enclosed in gardens behind its high stone wall. The only jarring element in that maximally efficient terrain is the gap-toothed arrangement that occasionally butts in, avenues of elegant mansions becoming mutantly interbred with distant, miniaturized cousins of the 1960s blocks of Vitry, as though to remind the shuddering residents of the nightmares that lie beyond its determinedly imagined borders. Like the extreme boundaries of Europe itself, that sense of enclosure is invisibly barricaded against contamination by projections of horror, fear and wealth. But the boundaries remain porous, eminently permeable to any invading force with superior vision.

In Neuilly, the suburban inhabitants' disdain for the sprawling city that lies on the far side of the peripheral road, intimately close, is at its most intense. As I approached the low snarl of that subterranean road from the sedate avenues, I passed along tree-shaded pathways that were erratically lined by the elderly residents of clinics, dazedly taking the air in faltering steps, and by children who smiled combatively at every unfamiliar passer-by, as though faced with a mysterious zoo animal which eluded categorization. The last mansions gave out; on the other side of the fast-moving channel, cut deep into the ground, I could see the image screens and advertising hoardings that marked the entrance to the city, and beyond them, the great monuments and boulevards, stretching down into its core. Finally, at the point where the beginning and end of my journey overlapped, I saw that there was no way in. The compulsive centrifugal movement of the peripheral journey had somehow acquired its own unbreakable momentum, separating out the vital memories, images and sensations of Europe. I turned back from the city's edge.

On the way back out to my journey's point of origin, I crossed the dream splinter of the Île de la Grande Jatte, which divides the river between Neuilly and La Défense. Stepping onto the island from a footbridge suspended over the rapidly flowing water, you are abruptly delivered from the imperative visual demands of the suburbs. The island's somnolent residents live on tarred houseboats moored around its steep banks, their jetties reached via rickety staircases of zigzagging planks; other, land-bound residents inhabit black wooden shacks that rest in creaking seclusion, half-submerged between the overhanging trees. As you walk along the narrow island, time slews away to a halt in decelerating heartbeats, and every conflicting memory and image is cancelled into oblivion. The encompassing presence of the river and the dripping trees permanently chill the air, and the body and eyes gradually cool into a state of suspended animation. That cryogenic state is interrupted only at the island's northern edge, from where the concrete apartment blocks of the northern suburbs reappear in the far distance, their blunt forms scattered across the low horizon, never erased, after all.

As I ascended the central promenade of La Défense as darkness was falling, from the river to the Grande Arche, the corporate towers lit up one by one. The last office workers were leaving for the night, funnelled into the subway station, and the shopping complexes disgorged the final straggling elements of their clientele onto the main plaza. A tower was under construction, screened by a huge hoarding which announced that a new storey would be added with each passing week, until its height surpassed that of all the others. The night sky began to glow with the towers' illumination, and

below the Grande Arche, a loose collection of figures was arranged along the steps, each staring down the esplanade in a direct perspective towards the Arc de Triomphe, miraculously visible within the boundaries of the city. As on the first night of my traversal of the city's periphery, I slipped away behind the Grande Arche to the jetty. A year on, it was still going nowhere, abandoned above the cemetery, its tip inhabited only by heated young lovers from the adjacent suburb. If, from all the innumerable images from that journey, I wanted only one to survive, and had to choose between those entangled human bodies or the panorama of the city's expelled edge, the only solution would be to melt the two together, in an image of digitally blurred exhilaration.

In extreme Europe, all images are annulled in their own excess and exhaustion. The essential visual traces of the twentieth century disappeared in a few moments at its end – the vital images were hammered and mutated into proliferating media material, which in its turn rapidly evanesced as it was consumed in gulps, gone forever along with the salutary meanings of terror and horror, of ecstasy and empathy. From that scorched-earth clearance of memory, any overlooked trace remains located far away on the perimeter of Europe and its cities, hidden in the cracks between the past and the future, heat-sealed and coated in ashes, its force magnified in visual ferocity by its isolation. Around the volatile borders of Europe, the powerful façade of media images stands at its most vulnerable, with every inflicted rip capable of precipi-tating a thunderous downfall of that screen into broken shards and echoes, its impact penetrating through to the heart of its cities, into silence and blackout. Europe lies on deeply seismic visual ground, the determining rhythm of its digital future reeling wildly between images and voids.

In Europe's breakdown zones of culture, around its cities and its far edges, all strategies of resistance are conceived, in perversity, within the engulfing atmosphere of expired tenement buildings and concrete-block terrains, where an overwhelming television lassitude has relentlessly extracted the life from vast populations of crumpled human figures. Every image exclaims its own status, and every media con-glomerate vaunts its own power, with such insistent repetition that exposed eyes are whipped into a blind focus around which all other sensory organs amass, deflated and drained. Other figures are cast out of that corralled visual equilibrium altogether, stumbling in narcotic disarray through the lost wastelands that constellate the suburbs, or else propelled into the political extremisms of Europe, each of which possesses

its own repetitious forms of visual power. A culture of resistance can only take the form of cancellation and negation, levelled against the image-coma of human life in contemporary Europe, and the eruptions of that resistance are intractably edged with fury, as every journey around Europe's periphery reveals. But the strange compulsions and contradictions that deeply underlie Europe guarantee that any aberrant resistance to its media power always mixes ferocious anger with pure caprice, caustic glares with elated vision.

Around the peripheries of Europe, the air is caught up in a storm of conflicting voices and languages. Eventually, one voice uproots another, or merges with it, or discovers a way to alternate with it. The edges of Europe and its cities are inhabited by a population of exiled presences: they are exiled from beyond its parameters, or else within their own countries, by upheaval, invasion or oppression. The homogenous image screens of Europe depend on a parallel unity of sound for their power – and any enforcement of the arbitrary limits of Europe pivots on the illusion of having a single texture, a solitary voice to fill the space that those limits encompass. But the ricocheting pulses of noise generated on the edges of Europe nonchalantly overwhelm such spurious ambitions. Europe is voiced into hybrid, multiple constellations of sound which drive vivid images of resuscitation along with them. The extreme peripheries of Europe are the domain in sensory flux of its exiles, whose visions for its future aim to dissolve its rigid prohibitions – and the unyielding faces of Europe's stultified cities carry the first impacts of that transformation.

All journeys into the extreme zones of Europe leave a virulent afterburn on the retina which eventually accumulates, line upon line, resolving itself into a lucid map. Europe closes in so rapidly upon the eye after revealing its momentary illuminations that every memory or image becomes fiercely highlighted against the encompassing darkness. Time is stilled on the endless traversals of Europe's wastelands, then suddenly accelerates into blood-pumping immediacy in the precarious night streets of its cities, where any act can reveal its contrary form in an instant. Space narrows on the terminally constricted edges with their populations of bodies pinioned between raw walls, then abruptly expands into gaping perspectives that stretch the contours of vision to the maximum. Moving around and through Europe, it seems that its urban terrain is one of permanent mishap, of malfunctioning digital images, of lost directions and of crashed myths. And on every journey, it becomes clear that Europe, the city and the eye are, all three, never centred: perpetually jarred, misplaced, obscured, they throw their vital matter aside, in sudden ejections, to be rescued and sifted through only later.

As you leave Europe behind, it recedes into a seething panorama of cities and bodies, of zones of heat and cold, of arrangements of images and texts. For a moment, as you ascend, everything holds its ground tenaciously; then it swiftly collapses into disarray. The power of Europe's media screens snaps off like a broken lightbulb. Its wastelands of abandoned debris and intricate concentrations of corporate towers melt into one another. The resolutely massing figures in the city streets are transformed into a vast, random scattering. The destitute concrete cities become indistinguishable from affluent cities of luxurious mansions. The pollution clouds hanging over the cities lose their noxious volume and turn transparent. All of the violent conflicts that inflame the peripheries of Europe deliquesce as though they were radiating only sensations of joy or ecstasy. Every national obsession, hallucination and myth seeps away into the air, and the borders and limits of Europe disappear, utterly annulled. The mountain ranges and lakes are relentlessly miniaturized and then dissolved by the onrushing impact of the other, far vaster continents. Europe fades away as you ascend. Though it leaves no memory, it retains its visual compulsion until the last moment. You keep watching, until the final traces evanesce and the words that form Europe vanish, one by one, into silence.

Acknowledgements

I would like to thank the Leverhulme Trust and the Getty Program, which provided me with grants to write this book; also Joe Kerr at the Royal College of Art, London, and Pierre Guyotat, with whom I made the journeys for the book's final part.

Photographic Acknowledgements

Page 21: Durrës, Albania in the time of Enver Hoxha. Photo: Barnaby's/Günter R. Reitz; 24: Istanbul: Galata Bridge and the texts of the city, 1960s. Photo: Barnaby's/S. B. Davie; 26: Istanbul demolition site, 2000. Photo: author; 32—3: Marseilles from Notre Dame de la Garde, 1960s. Photo: Barnaby's/Ken Lambert; 35: Marseilles and the origins of Western civilization, 2000. Photo: author; 39: Lisbon: the Alfama, early 1960s. Photo: Barnaby's/Ray Roberts; 40: Lisbon: the Alfama, 2000. Photo: author; 43: The end of Europe: Cabo da Roca, Portugal, 2000. Photo: author; 55: Chain gang of women at work clearing rubble, Berlin, 1945. Photo: Barnaby's/S. Ellis; 63: East Berlin's Alexanderplatz in the period of the GDR. Photo: Barnaby's/Col. Temple; 65: East Berlin cityscape in the period of the GDR. Photo: Barnaby's/Richard Gardner; 69: The Karlshorst capitulation museum in eastern Berlin, 2000. Photo: author; 70: The Karlshorst capitulation museum. Photo: author; 77: The Cecilienhof in Potsdam, 2000. Photo: author; 78: The Cecilienhof: the view from Stalin's window. Photo: author; 80: The Cecilienhof: graffiti carved in the lead of Stalin's window. Photo: author; 81: The Cecilienhof: Soviet army graffiti on the terrace. Photo: author; 82: The Soviet war memorial in Treptower Park in (the former East) Berlin, 2000. Photo: author; 85: Treptower Park: the ineradicable texts of Stalin. Photo: author; 90: Aubervilliers, on the outskirts of Paris, 2000. Photo: Reaktion Books; 95: CNIT building, La Défense, Paris, 2000. Photo: Reaktion Books; 96: La Défense, Paris, 2000. Photo: Reaktion Books; 99: View from La Défense, Paris, 2000. Photo: Reaktion Books; 105, 116—17: Aubervilliers, 2000. Photos: Reaktion Books; 122: La Grande Arche, La Défense, Paris, 2000. Photo: Reaktion Books; 124: La Jetée, La Défense, Paris, 2000. Photo: Reaktion Books.